SACRED
CHAKRAS

SACRED
CHAKRAS

VICTOR ARCHULETA

NEW BURLINGTON

A QUARTO BOOK

Published by
New Burlington Press
The Old Brewery
6 Blundell Street
London N7 9BH

ISBN: 978-0-85762-971-5

Conceived, edited and designed by
Quarto Publishing
an imprint of The Quarto Group
The Old Brewery
6 Blundell Street
London N7 9BH
www.quartoknows.com

QUAR: 336374

Editor & designer: Michelle Pickering
Editorial assistant: Charlene Fernandes
Illustrators: Kuo Kang Chen (sidebar icons),
Svetlana Voloshina (yoga/mudra/reiki poses)
Art director: Gemma Wilson
Publisher: Sam Warrington

Printed in Singapore

10 9 8 7 6 5 4 3 2 1

Contents

CAUTION

The information in this book is for educational
purposes only. It is not intended to replace
the advice of a doctor or medical practitioner.
Please see your healthcare provider before
beginning any new health programme.

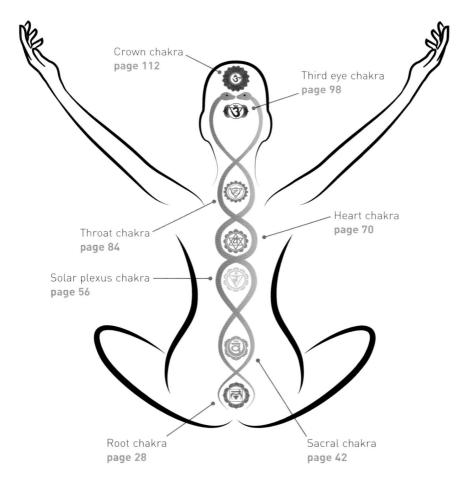

Introduction

Chakras are the body's energy centres and are key to physical health, emotional stability and mental clarity. Ensuring your chakras are perfectly balanced offers a new dimension of healing and growth.

In myriad ways, the systems of the human form connect and coalesce in the seven energy centres known as chakras. These are located in the head and along the spine. Generally, the understanding is that there are energetic pathways that spiral from the top of the head, down the spine to the sacrum and back up to the head. The back-and-forth spirals of energy flowing down and up the spine intersect at seven points – these are the chakras.

There are many body systems and esoteric systems that interact with the vitality of the chakra system. Each of the seven chakras corresponds to a physical neurologic ganglia or plexus along the spine at specific energetic points of intersection. These energy centres influence the function of nearby endocrine glands and organs and together they form the backbone of wellness.

THE IMPORTANCE OF BALANCED CHAKRAS

Each chakra energy centre can become out of balance and may cause other chakras to become out of balance as well. An overactive chakra needs to be calmed and reined in, while an underactive chakra needs to be energized and activated. This distinction will help bring awareness to the chakra to return it to a state of equilibrium.

Meditation, yoga, astrology, crystals, reiki energy therapy and conscious nutrition can be utilized to balance the energies of the chakras. Having an awareness of the interdependencies of these healing systems with the chakra system is useful in developing a self-awareness of the chakras and how they affect your well-being.

'There is a vitality, a life force, an energy, a quickening, that is translated through you into action, and because there is only one of you in all time, this expression is unique. And if you block it, it will never exist through any other medium and will be lost.' MARTHA GRAHAM

ABOUT
CHAKRAS

Chakras and the Body

The chakras are interconnected with physical health, including the functions of the major body systems, specific organs and parts of the body, and the endocrine glands.

Internal processes operate to keep the conditions in your body within tight limits, allowing metabolic chemical reactions to proceed. Homeostatic processes act at the level of the cell, the tissue and the organ, as well as for the organism as a whole.

If you are well acquainted with your own body, you may already know where you are physically out of balance in one or more areas. If so, you may begin to address some of the issues caused by stress or injuries acquired in your daily life. You only need to know what the corresponding chakra is for a particular physical system, organ or body part.

Chakra	Body systems*	Body parts/organs	Endocrine glands
Root	Gastrointestinal, reproductive, immune	Colon, anus, prostate, legs, feet	Adrenals – regulate metabolism and the immune system
Sacral	Gastrointestinal, urinary, reproductive	Pelvic area, kidneys, bladder, hips, reproductive organs	Testes/ovaries – regulate sexual development and secrete sex hormones
Solar plexus	Gastrointestinal	Abdomen, lower back, stomach, pancreas, spleen, liver, gallbladder, intestines	Pancreas – regulates metabolism
Heart	Respiratory, circulatory, immune	Thoracic cavity, heart, upper back, ribcage, chest, lungs	Thymus – regulates the immune system
Throat	Respiratory, circulatory, gastrointestinal, immune	Mouth, jaw, throat, vocal cords, neck, trachea, thyroid, shoulders, arms, hands	Thyroid – regulates body temperature and metabolism
Third eye	See below	Eyes, ears, nose, sinuses, hypothalamus, medulla	Pituitary – produces hormones that govern the function of the previous five glands; see also crown chakra
Crown	See below	Brain, cerebral cortex, cranium	Pineal – regulates biological cycles, including sleep; sometimes also linked to third eye chakra

*Nervous, musculoskeletal and endocrine body systems are influenced by all seven chakras

Ayurvedic Energy Flow and Kundalini Yoga

Chakra energy centres occur as spinning vortices and patterns that have been studied and documented in ancient Ayurvedic and Chinese medicine. Ayurveda is a system of medicine that emphasizes the mind's ability to influence the holistic healing and transformation of the body.

AYURVEDIC NAMES

- Root chakra: *Muladhara*
- Sacral chakra: *Svadhisthana*
- Solar plexus chakra: *Manipura*
- Heart chakra: *Anahata*
- Throat chakra: *Vishuddha*
- Third eye chakra: *Ajna*
- Crown chakra: *Sahasrara*

In Ayurveda, there are currents of energy – known as prana, chi or kundalini shakti – that move up and down the spine through the nadis (energy channels). The three nadis of Vedic scriptures are named ida, pingala and sushumna.

Ida and pingala are like two serpents coiled around a central core, sushumna. Together they form the shape of a caduceus, the symbol for healing in Western medical professions. It is interesting to note that it is also the shape of the double helix structure of molecular DNA.

AYURVEDIC PRINCIPLES

The nadis form the back-and-forth flow of kundalini energy up and down the spine and intersect at the first five chakras. The balancing of energetic flow of the ida (feminine) and pingala (masculine) currents contributes to the balancing of the first six chakras.

Having some knowledge of Ayurvedic philosophy provides a foundation for understanding the flow of energy between the seven chakras. This in turn provides an understanding of how kundalini energy is activated for specific chakra energy centres through kundalini yoga poses and mudra hand positions in meditation.

PINGALA

The pingala spiral current is associated with the energy of the sun and moves masculine attributes with a warming effect. Pingala is extroverted and corresponds to the left side of the brain and to the parasympathetic nervous system.

IDA

The ida spiral current is associated with the energy of the moon and moves feminine attributes with a cooling effect. Ida is introverted and corresponds to the right side of the brain and to the sympathetic nervous system.

SUSHUMNA

The sushumna current is the central channel running along the spinal cord and is associated with balance, stillness and the neutral mind. Kundalini energy rises from the root chakra through five chakras to the crown chakra via the sushumna. It is stabilizing and grounding, and corresponds to the central nervous system.

TATTVAS (ELEMENTS)

- Root chakra: *Earth*
- Sacral chakra: *Water*
- Solar plexus chakra: *Fire*
- Heart chakra: *Air*
- Throat chakra: *Ether*
- Third eye chakra: *All*
- Crown chakra: *All*

THE FLOW OF KUNDALINI ENERGY

The flow of kundalini energy has three distinct functions in yogic anatomy.

• Chakras 1 through 3 (root, sacral and solar plexus) comprise the lower triangle and are primarily concerned with the physical aspects of the body and the lower energetic frequencies.

• Chakras 5 through 7 (throat, third eye and crown) comprise the upper triangle and are primarily concerned with the accumulation of spiritual and higher energetic frequencies.

• Chakra 4 (heart) functions as the balancing point between the upper and lower triangles and is primarily concerned with the connecting of the physical, earthly energies to those of the spiritual, heavenly energies.

THE FIVE TATTVAS

The tattvas are the fundamental elements that make up everything in the universe, including ourselves. The five basic tattvas are the elements of density (earth), movement (water), heat (fire), flow (air) and spiritual connection (ether). Each tattva is associated with a chakra.

KUNDALINI YOGA

The practice of kundalini yoga provides a physical experience through asanas (body postures), mudras (hand positions and seals) and mantras (chants), as well as an energetic experience through the five tattvas (elements).

Together, these practices facilitate the rising of kundalini energy to bring about an awareness of the chakra energy centres. With this awareness, we have an opportunity to monitor which chakras are active and balanced and which are neutral or out of balance, and to awaken the energies of self-healing.

'Men of great knowledge actually found out about the chakras – their workings, their petals, their sounds, their infinity, their co-relationship, their powers. They found that the life of a human is totally based on these chakras. They developed into a whole science. This total science gave birth to kundalini yoga. That is how kundalini yoga was born.' YOGI BHAJAN

Meditations and Mantras

Meditation is a practice that allows you to ground yourself and to feel connected to the universal life energy. Meditation can take many forms, from simply focusing on your breathing to chanting a mantra.

MANTRAS

- Root chakra: *Lam*
- Sacral chakra: *Vam*
- Solar plexus chakra: *Ram*
- Heart chakra: *Yam*
- Throat chakra: *Ham*
- Third eye chakra: *Aum*
- Crown chakra: *Om*

A mantra is a word or phrase that influences the mind through its continuous repetition, or through constant focus upon it. It can be uttered silently or aloud, and plays a key part in many yogic practices, including meditation.

By focusing your energy and attention inwardly through meditation, you are able to obtain clarity and awareness of your thoughts and feelings without the distractions of the outside world. Clarity and awareness will provide the insight needed to balance chakras that may need attention.

BALANCING THE TENSION

If you are feeling low-energy/lethargic, focus your attention on the connection to the sky. Conversely, if you are feeling high-energy/anxious, focus on the connection to the centre of the earth. This will help balance the tension of grounding and connecting.

MEDITATION EXERCISE

It is helpful to do this exercise before engaging in any chakra balancing protocols. Trust that the process will work for your highest good, and allow the session to unfold without making it mean anything.

1   Set an intention for yourself. For example:

'I fill the space with golden light energy that is calming and nurturing.'

'I trust that the universal life energy will provide healing and vitalizing assistance to the receiver where it is needed.'

'I allow the universal life energy to move with ease through me to the receiver with no attachment to any particular result or outcome.'

2   Sit upright in a comfortable chair with both feet flat on the floor. Place your hands in prayer pose, with the heels of your palms and fingertips pressing against each other and the sides of your thumbs pressing against your chest.

3   Close your eyes, and gently press your tongue on the roof of your mouth, just behind your front teeth.

4   Perform long, deep breathing by slowly inhaling for eight seconds through your nose, allowing your belly to expand just below the navel, then gently exhaling through your nose for another eight seconds. Do this for three cycles (48 seconds).

5   Repeat the long, deep breathing cycle, but this time also hold your breath for five seconds at the end of each inhale and for five seconds at the end of each exhale. Do this for three cycles (78 seconds). Continue breathing comfortably at your own pace.

Astrology and the Chakras

As the planets move through the signs of the astrological zodiac, corresponding energetic associations occur within each of the seven major chakras of the human body. There are varying perspectives of how these associations are made, including the one described here.

POWER CHAKRAS

- Capricorn: *Root*
- Aquarius: *Root*
- Sagittarius: *Sacral*
- Pisces: *Sacral*
- Aries: *Solar plexus*
- Scorpio: *Solar plexus*
- Libra: *Heart*
- Taurus: *Heart*
- Gemini: *Throat*
- Virgo: *Throat*
- Cancer: *Third eye*
- Leo: *Crown*

Each chakra is associated with a particular astrological sign and its ruling planets. The first five chakras are associated with two zodiac signs each, and the last two chakras with one zodiac sign each. The astrological sign at your time of birth determines which of your seven chakras is the most powerful. This chakra is known as your power chakra, and may be thought of as your strong suit – the chakra that represents the energies that come to you most naturally.

SUPPORTING YOUR POWER CHAKRA

Your power chakra is your dominant chakra and is your main source of power. Understanding the different aspects of your zodiac sign may provide an understanding of how you or others move through life, and can provide context to the dynamic nature of the astrological influences that specifically affect your energetic body.

For example, if your zodiac sign is Libra, your desire for loving friendships and relationships is supported by the heart chakra. Your innate love of all things beautiful, as well as your desire for fairness and justice, are reinforced by the planet Venus, the goddess of love, desire and harmony.

The meditations and mantras associated with each chakra can be used as a tool to support your power chakra.

Diet, Teas and Tinctures

The health of the chakras influences the health of the body, and in turn is influenced by our diet. Proper food and nutrition are fundamental to our well-being. What we put into our bodies directly affects our health. Air, water and food are necessary to sustain life. Of the three, food offers the most variety of choices and provides fuel at different frequencies that correspond to the chakra energy centres.

TEAS

Plant parts can be used to make teas by decoction (boiling in water) or infusion (cold brews using water, oil or alcohol).

Nature provides food of varying colours and sources. Whether animal-based or vegetable-based, the choices we make have an effect on the chakras and body systems that we want to keep in equilibrium. Distinguishing which foods are associated with each chakra is helpful for maintaining chakra health and balance.

A HEALTHY DIET

To maintain a healthy lifestyle, it is extremely beneficial to commit to eating a diet comprised of whole, fresh, unprocessed and locally produced food. Without creating undue burden, strive to follow the 80/20 rule: attempt to eat healthy foods 80 per cent of the time and give yourself room to indulge in moderation 20 per cent of the time.

Create reasonable expectations for eating a healthy diet. Aim to choose from fresh, local, raw, organic sources. Processed, factory farmed, overcooked, genetically modified, antibiotic and pesticide infused food creates an unnecessary challenge for the body (and the earth) to overcome.

HEALING PLANTS AND HERBS

Along with the colour of the food, different parts of plants can provide energy that benefits different chakras. Roots, bark, stems, leaves, flowers and seeds all provide different nutrition that affects different chakras.

Indigenous people around the world have used plants and herbs as medicine to address ailments and disease for thousands of years. Plants and herbs can be used in cooking and, when made into teas or tinctures, to help connect us with nature and maintain a healthy mind, body and spirit.

TEAS AND TINCTURES

Herbal preparations such as teas and tinctures can help to detox the body and enhance its natural healing abilities. They can be stimulating or calming, energizing or relaxing, warming or cooling to the body. When properly used, these herbal preparations can help to lower blood pressure, blood sugar and cholesterol and reduce inflammation.

Nature's medicine in the form of herbs can also help to balance the flow of kundalini energy and clear physical, neurologic, circulatory or energetic blockages so that the optimum flow of energy is achieved.

TINCTURES

Tinctures are usually alcohol-based formulations of one or more herbs that concentrate the beneficial properties of the plant. Spagyric ('to draw out') tinctures are made using traditional alchemical processes.

Reiki Subtle Energy Therapy and Essential Oils

Reiki is a form of healing that was developed in Japan early in the twentieth century by Mikao Usui. Usui coined the term *reiki* to describe the concept of universal life energy.

A number of different methods of reiki have evolved. The Usui system is a form of reiki practice that allows the practitioner to have contact with the energy of reiki simply by laying on of hands in self-treatment and the treatment of others. By using hand positions on specific areas of the body, we can direct the universal life energy through the palms of the hands towards the chakra energy centres to facilitate balancing and equilibrium of the chakra system.

ESSENTIAL OILS

Essential oils are highly concentrated oils containing volatile compounds, and are distilled from various parts of medicinal plants and herbs. The waters that remain after the essential oils have been extracted during the distillation process are known as hydrosols. These contain minute amounts of essential oils and other water-soluble parts of the distilled plants and herbs.

Essential oils and hydrosols can be used alongside reiki to balance or activate the chakra energy centres. They can be applied to the soles of the feet and the back of the neck, or externally at the point of any of the seven chakras.

22

Crystal, Colour and Sound Therapies

Each chakra is associated with several crystals as well as specific colours and sounds. Crystals have long been used for a variety of wellness purposes. Colours and sounds are also beneficial to use during a crystal balancing session.

Singing bowls are a type of bell, with the rim vibrating to produce a harmonic sound when rung. They can be used as an aid to meditation along with crystals.

Crystals can be placed on your body, worn as parts of jewellery or carried in pouches to receive the benefits of their particular energetic frequencies. They can also be placed on the body or held in the hand while setting intentions, performing meditations and reciting affirmations and mantras for each of the seven chakras.

CHOOSING CRYSTALS

You may simply choose crystals that are the same colour as the chakra you would like to balance. Note that there are some crystals with specific properties that work with certain chakras even though the colour does not match the one associated with the chakra. The effectiveness is greatly influenced by your knowledge and intention.

COLOURS AND SOUNDS

There are a number of chakra balancing videos and music tracks available on the internet that provide sound and colour associated with each chakra. These can be helpful in stimulating multiple senses with frequencies and vibrations that help focus attention and intention to balance each chakra.

Chakra	Crystal	Colour	Musical note
Root	Garnet	Red	C
Sacral	Carnelian	Orange	D
Solar plexus	Citrine	Yellow	E
Heart	Rose quartz	Green	F
Throat	Aquamarine	Light blue	G
Third eye	Amethyst	Indigo	A
Crown	Clear quartz	Violet	B

NOTE: The crystals listed above are common crystals used for malas (prayer beads) for each chakra. Malas can be used while meditating on a specific chakra, and often contain 108 beads to count (track) the number of times that you repeat a mantra or practise a particular breathing sequence. Additional crystals are listed for each chakra in the directory.

CHAKRA
DIRECTORY

Root Chakra

The root or *muladhara* chakra is the first of the seven chakras and is the
first of three physical chakras. It is the foundation of the chakra system
and governs your feelings of safety, survival and security.

ROOT CHAKRA

The root chakra is located
near the perineum, at the
base of the spine between
the genitals and the anus.

The root chakra is the first chakra to develop in the womb
and in the first year of life. It drives your will to survive in
the material world. This energy centre powers your fight-or-
flight impulse. You are grounded and know when to run and
when to push back. When properly developed, you will feel
safe, nurtured and connected to yourself, your family and
your community.

The root chakra represents safety and connection and
links you to the physical world through the first of the
five Ayurvedic tattvas (elements), earth. This chakra
has an energetic colour of red and is symbolized by the
four-petal lotus.

BALANCED / UNBALANCED CONDITIONS

With a balanced first chakra you feel stable and have a
strong will to live based on feelings of courage and security.

Imbalances in the first chakra may leave you feeling spacey,
light-headed and even dizzy. These imbalances may be
situational or related to historical trauma, such as child
neglect, abuse and even a difficult birth. Chronic ailments
from the hips down may result. Because you are not
grounded in the physical world, you may be left with
feelings of impending danger and uncertainty.

If the root chakra is overactive, you may experience a sense of anxiety or paranoia. You may worry unnecessarily and be plagued by catastrophic thinking, such as fear of losing your job, home or relationship. The world around you will often seem chaotic and unmanageable. Because of feelings of scarcity, you may compensate by becoming greedy, arrogant, angry, competitive and judgemental, and see life as a zero-sum game of winners and losers.

If the root chakra is underactive, you may feel powerless and disconnected from the world, losing your ability to trust those around you. You may feel victimized in an 'us versus them' view of the world. You may even be afraid of the dark or afraid to be alone for no apparent reason. You may also be mistrusting and have feelings of low self-esteem, hopelessness and depression. As a result, you may even have suicidal thoughts, seeing no way out of situations you feel were imposed upon you.

Root chakra
The Body

BODY PARTS

- Tailbone
- Male reproductive organs
- Legs
- Feet

ENDOCRINE GLANDS

Adrenal glands – regulate
the metabolism and
immune system.

The major body systems associated with the root chakra are:

- **Musculoskeletal system:** Coccygeus muscles and muscles of the perineum, bones of the coccyx and sacrum

- **Nervous system:** Coccygeal plexus, spinal cord, peripheral nervous system, autonomic nervous system

- **Endocrine system:** Adrenal glands, gonads

- **Gastrointestinal system:** Rectum, anus

- **Reproductive system:** Reproductive organs

- **Immune system:** Adrenal glands

The root chakra is the base chakra and is located at the seat of the body. It is the foundation of the chakra system. It is the densest chakra and supports the physical infrastructure of the body (musculoskeletal system) as well as providing a grounding point for the body's electrical (nervous) system. The root chakra also provides support for the chemical infrastructure (endocrine system) of the body.

The biomechanics of the body depend on proper alignment of the musculoskeletal system. Physically, the pelvis supports the weight of the entire upper body and provides the pivot points for the femurs of the legs to carry the body by walking or running. A properly balanced pelvis allows the hips, knees, ankles, feet and toes to remain aligned for optimum biomechanics. If any of these joints are misaligned, then the alignment of all of the other joints, the spine and the head and shoulders will also be misaligned.

Maintaining a balanced root chakra contributes to the physical health of the lower pelvic girdle, legs and feet and enables us to be ambulatory to move about our world. Keeping the root chakra energized and vital will help to maintain the health of the organs of elimination, the reproductive organs and the associated body systems.

ADRENALS GLANDS AND THE ROOT CHAKRA

A balanced root chakra helps the adrenal glands regulate general metabolism and the immune system of the body. Healthy adrenal glands are foundational to the basic fight-or-flight response of the human body. The regulation of the hormones released by the adrenal glands ensures that the complex sequence of events that prepares the body for a serious confrontation or for escaping a dangerous situation is properly executed. If we keep these parts of our body in good working condition, we can look forward to independence and self-sufficiency well into old age.

Root chakra
Ayurvedic/Kundalini

CROW POSE

Step 1

Step 2

The root chakra is the first physical energy centre of the lower triangle of kundalini energy flow. It connects the survival of the physical body with the needs and desires of the physical world. This chakra is associated with the first Ayurvedic tattva (element), earth, and is where the Ayurvedic nadis (energy channels) intersect at the base of the chakra system. Strengthening the physical structures around the root chakra provides a foundation to support the sacral and solar plexus chakras (second and third physical chakras).

Practising the following kundalini yoga poses will fortify the root chakra. Using the mudra (hand position) during meditation will help you to ground and centre yourself and to balance the root chakra.

CROW POSE

Repeat the entire sequence three times, with 30 seconds of long and deep breathing between repeats.

1   Stand with your feet shoulder-width apart. Hold your arms in front of you at shoulder height with your palms facing downwards.

2   Squat down as far as you can, keeping your back straight and feet flat on the ground.

3   Begin long and deep breathing. Inhale slowly through the nose for five seconds, then exhale slowly through the nose for five seconds.

4   Repeat inhale/exhale five times and then come back to a standing position.

CHILD'S POSE

Repeat the entire sequence ten times. After each inhale/exhale, allow yourself to slowly and gently sink into the mat.

Step 2

1   Kneel on your mat with knees hip-width apart and the top of your feet flat on the mat with big toes almost touching each other.

2   Sit back onto the heels of your feet. Lean forwards and comfortably rest your forehead on the mat in front of you. Lay your arms next to your body with your palms facing upwards.

3   Begin long and deep breathing. Inhale slowly through the nose for five seconds, then exhale slowly through the nose for five seconds.

4   Feel the stretch along your spine and between your 'sit bones' as you allow the perineum (between the genitals and anus) to fully relax.

GYAN MUDRA

Hold the mudra and continue the meditation for at least 2–3 minutes and for up to 10 minutes.

GYAN MUDRA

You may recite the root chakra mantra or affirmation (see page 34) while holding the mudra.

1   Sit cross-legged with a straight spine and the back of your hands on your knees. Let the tips of the thumb and index finger touch. Focus your attention on the perineum (between the genitals and anus).

2   As you hold the gyan mudra, focus on your breath and do Kegel exercises. Squeeze the muscles between the anus and genitals as you exhale for five seconds, then relax the muscles as you inhale for five seconds.

Root chakra
Meditations and Mantras

ASTROLOGY

CAPRICORN

A balanced root chakra supports the Capricornian's innate confidence, responsibility and discipline.

AQUARIUS

A balanced root chakra supports the Aquarian's innate friendly and social nature.

Using meditation and mantras on the root chakra can be calming. Focusing your attention on your connection to the earth will help stabilize your thoughts and soothe your nervous system. When you feel safe and secure, you create a solid foundation to support the rest of the chakras.

While you meditate, you can recite affirmations aloud and focus on your breathing, or you can repeat a mantra in your mind for a few minutes while you quietly sit still in your meditation.

Begin long and deep breathing and begin to visualize chakra balancing energy spinning at the base of your spine. Using your mind's eye, 'see' the colour red spinning between your genitals and anus. This is your connection to the physical world. Trust and security rest here. Allow this energy to ground and centre you, leaving you feeling peaceful and whole.

MANTRA: LAM

Lam is a cleansing mantra. Meditating while chanting 'lam' helps to clear the root chakra of energy blockages that may restrict the energy flow to the higher chakras. It also allows you to open up to feelings of being connected and worthy.

AFFIRMATION

'My root chakra is my first energy centre and it functions to ground me energetically to the earth.

It is the source of my connection to the physical world. My trust and security rest here.'

Root chakra
Diet

TINCTURES

Dandelion root tincture supports the root chakra and may help you stay steady and grounded in times of upset.

The root chakra is fuelled by foods that support grounding and connection to the earth. The focus is on red-coloured foods, root vegetables and foods high in protein and minerals that are essential to our survival. Consuming foods that support the root chakra facilitates grounding and balancing so that nutrition is properly absorbed and waste and toxins are efficiently eliminated.

The following are suggestions for foods that can be incorporated into your diet for optimum root chakra health and vitality:

Vegetables: Carrots, potatoes, parsnips, radishes, beetroots, onions, turnips, sweet potatoes

Protein: Eggs, red meat, beans, lentils, tofu, quinoa, soy, peanut/almond/cashew butter

Grains: Buckwheat, bulgur wheat, whole oats

Fruit: Red apples, watermelon, pomegranates, berries

Herbs/spices: Garlic, ginger, chives, horseradish, hot paprika, cayenne, pepper, chilli

Select one or more of
the root chakra balancing
herbs and brew them with
sacred intention to be
physically connected to
the earth. These teas are
grounding and calming,
and provide an overall
feeling of well-being.

- Dandelion root
- Elderflower
- Rosemary
- Rooibos
- Hibiscus (left)
- Ginger
- Sage

Root chakra
Reiki

Step 1

Step 2

Reiki subtle energy can be beneficial for balancing the root chakra. The simple act of acknowledging this vulnerable chakra and sending calm and peaceful energy will contribute to feelings of security and well-being.

Use the root chakra meditation (see page 34) and visualize the reiki universal life energy flowing as you hold the following hand positions. You may do this sitting upright in a chair with your feet flat on the ground.

1   Close your eyes and cup your hands. With your palms facing you and your fingertips facing downwards and inwards, place your hands on your lower abdomen. Gently press the base of your palms on your hips.

2   Close your eyes and cup your hands. With your palms facing you and your fingertips pointing downwards and inwards, place your hands behind you, on the top and centre of your buttocks. Gently press your little fingers on your sacrum.

Hold each hand position and continue the meditation for 2–3 minutes. Begin long and deep breathing as you visualize the reiki universal life energy flowing from the palms of your hands towards the base of your abdomen.

Visualize the colour red spinning between your genitals and anus. This is your connection to the physical world. Trust and security rest here. Allow this energy to ground and centre you, leaving you feeling peaceful and whole.

38

These essential oils have a 'green' or earthy scent that will help ground your root chakra. Dilute by mixing 1–2 drops of one or more of these essential oils with 5–6 drops of coconut oil. Rub this on the soles of your feet or the back of your neck, or externally at the point of the chakra.

- Vetiver
- Marjoram
- Myrrh
- Clove (left)

Root chakra
Crystals

COLOUR THERAPY

RED
⸻

The frequency of the colour red is in harmony with the frequency of the root chakra. Whether it is a red object or a red light, the root chakra will be affected. Red signifies caution or alerts you to a threat to your safety.

The frequency and resonance of root chakra crystals can help to ground you to the physical earth and provide the root chakra with the stability and connection needed to support the other six chakras. This is the seat of the chakra system and both the energetic resonance of the musical note C and the colour red enhance the frequencies of root chakra crystals.

The root chakra can be influenced by the energetic frequencies of any of the following crystals:

- Garnet
- Ruby
- Red jasper
- Fire agate
- Shungite
- Tiger's eye
- Hematite
- Black tourmaline
- Obsidian
- Onyx

Choose one or more of the crystals for balancing the root chakra. Simply hold the crystals in your left hand. Use the root chakra meditation (see page 34) for 3–5 minutes to send healing energy from the crystal to the root chakra energy centre. During your meditations, visualize the colour red and use recorded music or videos that support root chakra balancing.

40

SOUND THERAPY

NOTE C

Crystal bowls, singing
bowls, tuning forks and
gongs tuned to the note C
can be used alongside
crystals to balance the root
chakra. The note C will help
create a sense of security
and connection to the earth.

ABOVE (FROM TOP): Red jasper, tiger's eye
and black onyx are all crystals associated
with healing and unblocking the root chakra.
To determine which ones work best for you,
try out a couple and trust your intuition.

41

Sacral Chakra

The sacral or *svadhisthana* chakra is the second of the seven chakras and is the second physical chakra. It is the seat of creativity in your chakra system. It governs your feelings of pleasure and physical love and sexuality.

SACRAL CHAKRA

The sacral chakra is located just below the navel, at the centre of the lower abdomen, in front of the sacrum.

The sacral chakra is where creative energy flows to create and maintain healthy physical relationships through physical touch. This energy centre drives your will to create and your ability to move with the changes of the world around you. When properly developed, you 'go with the flow' of life and easily create material abundance and feelings of pleasure and joy.

The sacral chakra represents the fluid and flowing nature of life and links you to the physical world through the second of the five Ayurvedic tattvas (elements), water. This chakra has an energetic colour of orange and is symbolized by the six-petal lotus.

BALANCED / UNBALANCED CONDITIONS

With a balanced second chakra you feel creative and are able to comfortably express your sexuality.

Imbalances in the second chakra may leave you feeling guilty or shameful, particularly in the area of your sexuality. Sexual abuse or trauma may result in internalized anger that leaves you with blocked feelings and emotions. Relationships may be unstable and unbalanced, and you may be unable to allow the flow of abundance and success. Self-sabotage and self-criticism may prevent you from moving forward in life and you may blame yourself for not doing so.

**If the sacral chakra
is overactive,** you may experience
sexual compulsions or addictions.
You may be jealous or possessive
in your relationships, or move
from one physical relationship
to the next without regard to an
emotional connection. You may
seek even more physical pleasure
to overcome your feelings of guilt
and frustration.

If the sacral chakra is underactive,
you may feel shut down and stiff or
even frigid in your sexual relationships.
Issues of impotence or infertility may arise
as well as physical diseases of the pelvis.
Depression and internalized shame may keep you
from enjoying sexual relationships at all. You may be
numb and unable to feel happiness and joy as a result
of past or ongoing sexual abuse or trauma.

Sacral chakra
The Body

BODY PARTS

- Lower abdomen
- Pelvis
- Large intestine
- Female reproductive organs

ENDOCRINE GLANDS

Testes/ovaries – regulate sexual development and secrete sex hormones.

The major body systems associated with the sacral chakra are:

- **Nervous system:** Lumbar plexus, spinal cord, peripheral nervous system, autonomic nervous system

- **Musculoskeletal system:** Lower abdominal and oblique muscles, hip flexors, sacrum, lower lumbar spine

- **Endocrine system:** Gonads

- **Gastrointestinal system:** Sigmoid colon, rectum

- **Urinary system:** Kidneys, ureters, urinary bladder, urethra

- **Reproductive system:** Ovaries, fallopian tubes, uterus, vagina, testes, prostate, penis

The sacral chakra is located in the lower abdomen and sits on the foundation of the root chakra. This chakra vibrates at a higher frequency than the root chakra and generates the fluid movement of energy to support elimination and procreation. The reproductive organs, pelvic girdle and organs of elimination are energetically maintained by the sacral chakra.

The sacral chakra innervates the tissues and organs of the pelvis, including the male and female reproductive organs. The primary physical function of the sacral chakra is movement and sensation. A properly balanced sacral chakra ensures proper voiding of the urinary bladder, sigmoid colon and rectum. The healthy functioning of the testes and ovaries is necessary to create sperm and egg cells and to maintain hormonal balance and secondary sex characteristics. The reproductive system depends on an intricate movement of sperm and egg cells from their point of germination in the testes and ovaries to the point of conception near the fallopian tubes.

44

Maintaining a balanced sacral chakra provides the flow needed for the process that creates new life. Keeping the sacral chakra energized and vital will help maintain the health of the organs of elimination, the reproductive organs and the associated body systems.

TESTES/OVARIES (GONADS) AND THE SACRAL CHAKRA

A balanced sacral chakra helps the gonads regulate the primary sex hormones testosterone and oestrogen, which are created by the testes and ovaries respectively. The regulation of the sex hormones released by the reproductive glands ensures that the intricate sequence of events that the body undergoes prior to and during the sex act can occur with great efficiency and pleasure. If we keep our reproductive glands healthy and vital, we can look forward to a healthy and robust sex life well into old age.

Sacral chakra
Ayurvedic/Kundalini

Step 1

Step 2

The sacral chakra is the second physical energy centre of the lower triangle of kundalini energy flow. It connects the reproduction of the physical body with the survival of the species. This chakra is associated with the second Ayurvedic tattva (element), water, and is where the Ayurvedic nadis (energy channels) intersect below the navel. Strengthening the pelvis and reproductive organs around the sacral chakra provides a fluid container for movement and creativity.

Practising these kundalini yoga poses will fortify the sacral chakra. Using the mudra (hand position) during meditation will help to open the flow of energy and balance the sacral chakra.

FROG POSE

Repeat the entire sequence twice, with 1 minute of long and deep breathing between repeats.

1   Squat down, balancing on your toes with your knees apart and your heels together and off the floor. Hold your head high and place your fingertips on the floor in front of you between your knees.

2   Keep your fingertips on the floor and inhale slowly through the nose as you straighten your knees and lower your head in front of you. Straighten your knees as much as possible, keeping your heels lifted off the floor and your head as close to your knees as possible.

3   Exhale through the nose as you squat down and lift your head.

4   Repeat seven times and then return to a squat.

SUFI GRIND POSE

Repeat the entire sequence twice. Between repeats, sit upright and do 1 minute of long and deep breathing.

1   Sit cross-legged with a straight spine and hold your knees with your hands.

2   Begin rotating your spine in a clockwise motion by arching forwards and then slowly rotating to the right (A), then arching backwards and then slowing rotating to the left (B). Complete the rotation by arching forwards once again.

3   Continue this rotation for 2–3 minutes, keeping your head as still as possible.

4   Repeat this pose in an anticlockwise direction for 2–3 minutes.

SUFI GRIND POSE

Step 2A

Step 2B

DHYANI MUDRA

Hold the mudra and continue the meditation for at least 2–3 minutes and for up to 10 minutes.

1   Sit cross-legged with a straight spine. With the palms of your hands facing up and the fingertips pointing in opposite directions, place your left hand under your right and let the left palm touch the back of the fingers of the right hand, gently allowing the tips of the thumbs to touch.

2   As you hold the mudra just below your navel, focus on your breath. Slowly inhale for five seconds, hold for five seconds and then exhale for five seconds, keeping your belly relaxed. Let your diaphragm do the work, not your abdominal muscles. Do this for ten cycles.

DHYANI MUDRA

You may recite the sacral chakra mantra or affirmation (see page 48) while holding the mudra.

Sacral chakra
Meditations and Mantras

ASTROLOGY

SAGITTARIUS

A balanced sacral chakra supports forward movement for the Sagittarian's free-spirited quest for adventure.

PISCES

A balanced sacral chakra helps to nourish the Piscean's go-with-the-flow attitude.

Using meditation and mantras on the sacral chakra can be pleasurable and nurturing. Focusing your attention on your ability to feel energy in motion and physical intimacy will bring feelings of well-being and self-worth. When you feel the flow of creativity and acknowledge the sacredness of your sexuality, the rest of the chakras are also free to flow.

While you meditate, you can recite affirmations aloud and focus on your breathing, or you can repeat a mantra in your mind for a few minutes while you quietly sit still in your meditation.

Begin long and deep breathing and begin to visualize chakra balancing energy spinning at the centre of your pelvis. Using your mind's eye, 'see' the colour orange spinning just below your navel. This is the source of your creativity and inspiration. Your sexual desire and passion are born here. Allow this energy to flow freely with joy and respect for your gift of creation.

MANTRA: VAM

Vam is a healing mantra. Meditating while chanting 'vam' helps to heal the sacral chakra physically, emotionally and spiritually. It also facilitates flexibility, which allows energy to stay in motion.

AFFIRMATION

'My sacral chakra is my second energy centre and it functions to stimulate my child-like emotions and adventure.

It is the source of my creativity and inspiration. My sexual desire and passion are born here.'

Sacral chakra
Diet

Calendula tincture supports the sacral chakra and can help to brighten your creativity and lightheartedness.

The sacral chakra is fuelled by foods that support sensuality, movement, balance and pleasure. The focus is on orange-coloured foods, fruits, nuts, fish and chicken. These are all foods that get our creative juices moving. Consuming foods that support the sacral chakra facilitates the flow of emotions and the desire to create and have fun.

The following are suggestions for foods that can be incorporated into your diet for optimum sacral chakra health and vitality:

Protein: Fish, chicken

Fruit: Melons, mangos, strawberries, passion fruit, oranges, coconut

Herbs/spices: Cinnamon, vanilla, carob, sweet paprika, ginger

Nuts/seeds: Almonds, walnuts, cashews, sesame seeds, caraway seeds

Sweets: Raw honey

TEAS

Select one or more of the
sacral chakra balancing
herbs and brew them with
sacred intention to
facilitate movement and
elimination. These teas
are warming and
sensuous, and bring about
a sense of blissful joy.

- Calendula (left)
- Gardenia
- Hibiscus
- Liquorice
- Fennel

Sacral chakra
Reiki

Step 1

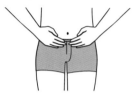

Step 2

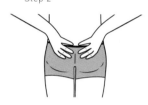

Reiki subtle energy can be beneficial for balancing the sacral chakra. Focusing your intention and energy on this fluid and sensual chakra will contribute to feelings of sweet pleasure.

Use the sacral chakra meditation (see page 48) and visualize the reiki universal life energy flowing as you hold these hand positions. You may do this sitting upright in a chair with your feet flat on the ground.

1   Close your eyes and cup your hands. With your palms facing you and your fingertips pointing towards each other, place your hands on your middle abdomen. Gently press your hands just below the navel.

2   Close your eyes and cup your hands. With your palms facing you and your fingertips pointing towards each other, place your hands behind you, on the lower part of your back. Gently press the base of your palms on your waist.

Hold each hand position and continue the meditation for 2–3 minutes. Begin long and deep breathing as you visualize the reiki universal life energy flowing from the palms of your hands towards the centre of your body.

Visualize the colour orange spinning just below your navel. This is the source of your creativity and inspiration. Your sexual desire and passion are born here. Allow your energy to flow freely with joy and respect for your gift of creation.

Use these rich, earthy and intoxicating scents to unlock the sweet pleasure of the sacral chakra. Dilute by mixing 1–2 drops of one or more of these essential oils with 5–6 drops of coconut oil. Rub this on the soles of your feet or the back of your neck, or externally at the point of the chakra.

- Sandalwood (left)
- Patchouli
- Ylang ylang

Sacral chakra
Crystals

COLOUR THERAPY

ORANGE

The frequency of the colour orange is in harmony with the frequency of the sacral chakra. Whether it is an orange object or an orange light, the sacral chakra will be affected. Orange is like the sun and signifies warmth and the sweet source of creation.

The frequency and resonance of sacral chakra crystals can facilitate flow for elimination and movement for reproduction. This is the chakra of sacred sexuality and both the energetic resonance of the musical note D and the colour orange enhance the frequencies of sacral chakra crystals.

The sacral chakra can be influenced by the energetic frequencies of any of the following crystals:

- Carnelian
- Orange calcite
- Sunstone

Choose one or more of the crystals for balancing the sacral chakra. Simply hold the crystals in your left hand. Use the sacral chakra meditation (see page 48) for 3–5 minutes to send healing energy from the crystal to the sacral chakra energy centre. During your meditations, visualize the colour orange and use recorded music or videos that support sacral chakra balancing.

SOUND THERAPY

NOTE D

Crystal bowls, singing
bowls, tuning forks and
gongs tuned to the note D
can be used alongside
crystals to balance the
sacral chakra. The note D
will help create a sense
of receiving inspiration
for creation.

ABOVE (FROM TOP): Carnelian, orange calcite
and sunstone are all crystals associated with
healing and unblocking the sacral chakra.
To determine which ones work best for you,
try out a couple and trust your intuition.

Solar Plexus Chakra

The solar plexus or *manipura* chakra is the third of the seven chakras and is the third physical chakra. It is the core of personal power in your chakra system. It governs your self-esteem, self-acceptance and self-reliance.

SOLAR PLEXUS CHAKRA

The solar plexus chakra is located just above the navel, at the centre of the upper abdomen, below the diaphragm.

The solar plexus chakra is where the heat needed to transform your food into fuel and energy is generated. This energy is used by your body to accomplish everyday maintenance, healing and to accommodate change. It is your energetic core and drives your will to take action. When properly developed, it enables your inner warrior to propel you forwards to overcome challenges.

The solar plexus chakra represents the heat and energy needed to facilitate transformation and links you to the physical world through the third of the five Ayurvedic tattvas (elements), fire. This chakra has an energetic colour of yellow and is symbolized by the ten-petal lotus.

BALANCED / UNBALANCED CONDITIONS

With a balanced third chakra you feel invincible and able to power through any obstacles or challenges.

Imbalances in the third chakra may leave you filled with doubt, self-hatred and a sense of inadequacy. These feelings may affect your ability to take charge and make decisions. Because of your lack of self-respect, you may give away your power and be left with internalized anger and resentment. This may lead to insensitivity to others. You may move through the world with extreme responses to minor annoyances.

If the solar plexus chakra is overactive, you may experience violent outbursts and an intolerance of others and even bullying. You may blame others for your mistakes and have a difficult time taking responsibility for your actions. An exaggerated sense of self may leave you with a need to look good and be right about everything. You may use your vanity and need for prestige to overpower and control those around you.

If the solar plexus chakra is underactive, you may feel intimidated and victimized by the world. Your poor self-image may leave you paralyzed and unable to take action. The heat or 'fire' generated by your solar plexus may be insufficient to sustain you with the energy needed to create a life you love. Your lack of confidence and self-doubt may leave you with a diminished sense of self. This may result in feelings of worthlessness and wanting to withdraw or disconnect from the world.

Solar plexus chakra
The Body

BODY PARTS

- Upper abdomen
- Lower back
- Small intestine
- Digestive system

ENDOCRINE GLANDS

Pancreas – regulates
metabolism.

The major body systems associated with the solar plexus chakra are:

- **Nervous system:** Solar plexus, spinal cord, vagus nerve, autonomic nervous system
- **Musculoskeletal system:** Upper abdominal and oblique muscles, diaphragm, lumbar spine
- **Endocrine system:** Pancreas
- **Gastrointestinal system:** Stomach, small intestine, pancreas, liver, gallbladder

The solar plexus chakra is located in the upper abdomen and affects the health of the liver, spleen, gallbladder and pancreas. A severe blow to this region can cause the diaphragm to spasm and result in getting the 'wind knocked out of you'.

A balanced solar plexus chakra helps ensure that the complex process needed to ensure the proper breakdown of food for metabolism and absorption can occur. The gallbladder provides bile and the pancreas provides digestive enzymes critical for proper digestion. The muscles of the stomach are used to break down the food we eat into a form that can then be further metabolized and absorbed in the small intestine. All of this movement is facilitated by the precisely timed peristaltic contraction and relaxation of the small intestine.

Maintaining a balanced solar plexus chakra literally provides the fuel needed to power your body at the cellular level. Keeping the solar plexus chakra energized and vital will benefit the digestive system and the associated body systems.

PANCREAS AND THE SOLAR PLEXUS CHAKRA

A balanced solar plexus chakra helps the pancreas produce the hormones needed to regulate blood sugar levels. Insulin, glucagon, somatostatin and pancreatic polypeptide are produced in the 'islets of Langerhans' within the pancreas. Overtaxing the pancreas by consuming excessive amounts of refined sugars can affect its ability to regulate blood sugar levels in the bloodstream and result in a form of diabetes. Diabetes can lead to a number of serious vascular complications detrimental to health. A healthy and vital pancreas will contribute to the health of your circulatory system and overall well-being.

Solar plexus chakra
Ayurvedic/Kundalini

CAT-COW POSE

Step 1

Step 2

The solar plexus chakra is the third physical energy centre of the lower triangle of kundalini energy flow. It connects the power of the solar plexus with the physical energy to take action. This chakra is associated with the third Ayurvedic tattva (element), fire, and is where the Ayurvedic nadis (energy channels) intersect above the navel. Strengthening the abdominals and middle back provides the support needed to do physical work to accomplish your goals.

Practising these kundalini yoga poses will fortify the solar plexus chakra. Using the mudra (hand position) during meditation will help to generate the fire needed to fuel the solar plexus chakra.

CAT-COW POSE

Repeat the entire sequence twice, resting between repeats by sitting back onto your heels and placing your forehead on the mat with your arms at your sides.

1   Get on all fours with hands at shoulder width and knees at hip width. Inhale deeply as you lift your head towards the ceiling and arch your back towards the floor. Keep your eyes open, gazing up; relax your abdominal muscles. (Cat pose)

2   Exhale fully as you arch your back towards the ceiling and move your head down, bringing your chin towards your chest. Keep your eyes open, gazing down, and tighten your abdominal muscles. (Cow pose)

3   Start slowly and evenly moving between the cat pose and cow pose, and build up your speed as much as feels comfortable. Continue for 2–3 minutes.

STRETCH POSE

Repeat the entire sequence twice, with 1–2 minutes of long and deep breathing between repeats.

Step 2

1. Lay on your back on the floor, with feet together and arms by your side.

2. Lift your arms off the floor with palms facing your thighs. Point your toes as you raise your heels and your head 15cm (6in) off the floor.

3. Gazing at your toes, begin rapid breathing through the nose by inhaling and exhaling 25 times. Then relax for five seconds.

4. Repeat five times and relax.

Note: Do not perform the stretch pose if pregnant or in the first week of a woman's moon cycle.

TANIT MUDRA

Hold the mudra and continue the meditation for at least 2–3 minutes and for up to 10 minutes.

TANIT MUDRA

1. Sit cross-legged with a straight spine. Press your hands together with fingers straight, the tips of your fingers touching and thumbs crossed right over left. Point your fingers forwards with the heels of your hands just above the navel.

2. As you hold the mudra just above your navel, focus on your breath. Slowly inhale for five seconds, hold for five seconds and then exhale for five seconds, keeping your belly relaxed. Let your diaphragm do the work, not your abdominal muscles. Do this for ten cycles.

You may recite the solar plexus chakra mantra or affirmation (see page 62) while holding the mudra.

Solar plexus chakra
Meditations and Mantras

ASTROLOGY

ARIES

A balanced solar plexus chakra provides Arians with the physical energy needed to fuel their leadership and entrepreneurial spirit.

SCORPIO

A balanced solar plexus chakra supports Scorpios with the action, focus, direction and ambition to explore the secrets and mysteries of life, sex and death.

Using meditation and mantras on the solar plexus chakra can be invigorating and inspiring. Focusing your attention on the heat in your belly will bring feelings of confidence and accomplishment. It provides you with the energy needed to take action and move powerfully in the world.

While you meditate, you can recite affirmations aloud and focus on your breathing, or you can repeat a mantra in your mind for a few minutes while you quietly sit still in your meditation.

Begin long and deep breathing and begin to visualize chakra balancing energy spinning at centre of your abdomen. Using your mind's eye, 'see' the colour yellow spinning just above your navel. This is the core of your power, the source of your wisdom and your 'gut feeling'. Allow this energy to fire you up to accomplish your goals.

MANTRA: RAM

Ram is a protective mantra. Meditating while chanting 'ram' helps to stoke the heat that will bring your dreams to fruition. It will stimulate your personal power and provide you with the enthusiasm and inspiration needed to excel as a leader, team player or artist.

AFFIRMATION

'My solar plexus chakra is my third energy centre and it functions to provide me with focus and power.

It is the source of my confidence and self-esteem. My gut feelings are sensed here.'

Solar plexus chakra
Diet

TINCTURES

Marshmallow root tincture supports the solar plexus chakra and can help to balance energetic flow and soften dense tension and anxiety.

The solar plexus chakra is fuelled by foods that support physical and emotional action. The focus is on yellow-coloured foods, grains, spices, teas, dairy and foods that provide us with the complex carbohydrates and healthy fats that will power and sustain our drive to succeed. Consuming foods that support the solar plexus chakra facilitates the long, slow burn that will provide the endurance needed to achieve your goals.

The following are suggestions for foods that can be incorporated into your diet for optimum solar plexus chakra health and vitality.

Grains: Pasta, cereal, rice, bread (consume whole grains, avoid white processed flour)

Nuts/seeds: Flax seeds, sunflower seeds, nuts, chia seeds

Herbs/spices: Cayenne, peppermint, spearmint, melissa, camomile, turmeric, cumin, fennel, anise, coriander

Dairy: Milk, cheeses, yoghurt (consume organic dairy products, avoid diary products from animals treated with hormones and antibiotics)

Select one or more of
the solar plexus chakra
balancing herbs and brew
them with sacred intention
to feel bright and
energized. These herbs
stimulate the taste buds
and provide you with
robust energy to propel
you through your life.

- Rosemary
- Ginger
- Anise
- Bergamot
- Peppermint (left)
- Fennel
- Cinnamon

Solar plexus chakra
Reiki

Step 1

Step 2

Reiki subtle energy can be beneficial for balancing the solar plexus chakra. Focusing your intention on this core energy centre will facilitate your ability to powerfully take action and fulfil your life goals and desires.

Use the solar plexus chakra meditation (see page 62) and visualize the reiki universal life energy flowing as you hold these hand positions. You may do this sitting upright in a chair with your feet flat on the ground.

1   Close your eyes and cup your hands. With your palms facing you and the tips of your middle fingers touching, place your hands on your upper abdomen. Gently press your palms on the bottom of your ribcage.

2   Close your eyes and cup your hands. With your palms facing you and your fingertips pointing towards each other, place your hands behind you, on the middle part of your back. Gently press your palms on the bottom of your ribcage.

Hold each hand position and continue the meditation for 2–3 minutes. Begin long and deep breathing as you visualize the reiki universal life energy flowing from the palms of your hands towards the centre of your body.

Visualize the colour yellow spinning in your solar plexus. This is the core of your power, the source of your wisdom and your gut feelings. Your drive and endurance are sourced here. Allow this energy to propel you to success.

Inhale the bright and motivating power of yellow sunlight to energize your solar plexus chakra and help your physical body spring into action. Dilute by mixing 1–2 drops of one or more of these essential oils with 5–6 drops of coconut oil. Rub this on the soles of your feet or the back of your neck, or externally at the point of the chakra.

- Camomile
- Lemon (left)
- Thyme

Solar plexus chakra
Crystals

COLOUR THERAPY

YELLOW

The frequency of the colour yellow is in harmony with the frequency of the solar plexus chakra. Whether it is a yellow object or a yellow light, the solar plexus chakra will be affected. Yellow signifies caution and yielding as you move powerfully through life.

The frequency and resonance of solar plexus chakra crystals can help vitalize the power of your physical core. This is the chakra of 'walking the talk' – taking action that supports the beliefs and passions you share with others. Both the energetic resonance of the musical note E and the colour yellow enhance the frequencies of solar plexus chakra crystals.

The sacral chakra can be influenced by the energetic frequencies of any of the following crystals:

- Citrine
- Yellow jasper
- Topaz

Choose one or more of the crystals for balancing the solar plexus chakra. Simply hold the crystals in your left hand. Use the solar plexus chakra meditation (see page 62) for 3–5 minutes to send healing energy from the crystal to the solar plexus chakra energy centre. During your meditations, visualize the colour yellow and use recorded music or videos that support solar plexus chakra balancing.

SOUND THERAPY

NOTE E

Crystal bowls, singing
bowls, tuning forks and
gongs tuned to the note E
can be used alongside
crystals to balance the
solar plexus chakra. The
note E will help create
a sense of confidence
and trust.

ABOVE (FROM TOP): Topaz, yellow jasper, and
citrine are all crystals associated with healing
and unblocking the solar plexus chakra.
To determine which ones work best for you,
try out a couple and trust your intuition.

69

Heart Chakra

The heart or *anahata* chakra is the fourth of the seven chakras and connects the lower three physical chakras with the upper three spiritual chakras. It is the gateway to your spiritual connection to the divine.

HEART CHAKRA

The heart chakra is located at the centre of the chest between the sternum and spine.

The heart chakra is where the love you have for yourself and others is generated. You are connected to your self in a deep way. This energy centre is the source of your ability to love and be loved. It bridges the connection to the lower three chakras and keeps you grounded and connected to your higher self. When properly developed, you are motivated by love and are able to generate joy, compassion and empathy in your life. You easily see the beauty in yourself and others.

The heart chakra represents the highest vibration in the physical realm and links you to the physical world through the fourth of the five Ayurvedic tattvas (elements), air. This chakra has an energetic colour of green and is symbolized by the twelve-petal lotus.

BALANCED / UNBALANCED CONDITIONS

With a balanced fourth chakra you feel self-love and love for others, you cannot be harmed or harm others and you can be of service with compassion and respect.

Imbalances in the fourth chakra may leave you feeling disconnected from yourself and others. You may have feelings of unprocessed grief or sorrow that leave you depressed or lonely. This may leave you resentful and angry and make relationships very challenging. You may give love where it is not deserved or wanted.

If the heart chakra is overactive, you may exhibit co-dependent tendencies and be easily hurt by the actions of others. You may consider the needs of others ahead of your own and may take on the emotions or problems of others. This may result in a misguided sense of what love is and lead to being overly affectionate and smothering your partner or your children with what you think is love. You may respond with passive-aggressive behaviour or being overly critical of others.

If the heart chakra is underactive, you may find it hard to engage in a romantic relationship. Because of your lack of self-love, you may be unable to experience the deep connection needed to cultivate and maintain a love relationship. Unable to trust others, you may shut down emotionally and question your own worthiness and desire to live a life filled with joy and satisfaction.

Heart chakra
The Body

- Thorax
- Upper back
- Lungs
- Ribcage
- Heart

ENDOCRINE GLANDS

Thymus – regulates the
immune system.

The major body systems associated with the heart
chakra are:

- **Respiratory system:** Lungs, bronchus

- **Circulatory system:** Heart and major blood vessels,
pulmonary arterioles, venules and capillaries

- **Nervous system:** Brachial plexus, spinal cord,
vagus nerve, peripheral nervous system, autonomic
nervous system

- **Musculoskeletal system:** Diaphragm, intercostal muscles,
heart, trapezius, spine, ribs

- **Endocrine system:** Thymus

- **Immune system:** Thymus, lymph vessels, lymph nodes

The heart chakra is located at the centre of the chest near
the heart and affects the heart, lungs, diaphragm and
thoracic spine. This is where blood is pumped through the
lungs to eliminate carbon dioxide and then circulate freshly
oxygenated blood through every blood vessel and capillary in
every tissue of the body.

The heart chakra energetically affects the major body
functions of respiration and circulation. A balanced heart
chakra helps ensure that the diaphragm regularly and
consistently contracts and relaxes automatically to inflate
and deflate the lungs, assuring a fresh supply of oxygen and
effective elimination of carbon dioxide. The heart muscle
in turn assures that every red blood cell of the body is
circulated through the lungs and delivered to virtually
every cell of the body.

Maintaining a balanced heart chakra assures that the primary mechanical functions of breath and heartbeat operate without fail through your entire life. Keeping the heart chakra energized and vital will benefit your respiratory and circulatory systems as well as the associated body systems.

THYMUS AND THE HEART CHAKRA

A balanced heart chakra helps the thymus produce the hormone thymosine, which is needed to stimulate the development and production of T-cells for the immune system. The production of T-cells ensures that the body will be able to fight off infectious diseases. The thymus is active and largest in childhood, and slowly shrinks and turns into fat after puberty. Once the T-cells have been created they migrate to the lymphatic system, where they are stored until needed for fighting infections and diseases. A healthy and vital thymus, especially in childhood, will provide your immune system with the disease-fighting lymphocytes that will protect you throughout your lifetime.

Heart chakra
Ayurvedic/Kundalini

CHEST FLY POSE

Step 1

The heart chakra is the balancing point between the lower and upper triangles of kundalini energy flow. It is the point at which the three physical chakras meet the three spiritual chakras. This chakra is associated with the fourth Ayurvedic tattva (element), air, and is where the Ayurvedic nadis (energy channels) intersect at the centre of the chest. Expanding the ribcage with deep breathing and lifting and opening the chest creates space to hold all of life in deep love.

Practising these kundalini yoga poses will fortify the heart chakra. Using the mudra (hand position) during meditation will help to facilitate the integration of lower and higher energies to balance the heart chakra.

CHEST FLY POSE

Repeat the entire sequence twice, with 1–2 minutes of long and deep breathing between repeats.

1   Sit cross-legged with a straight spine and lift your arms straight to the sides, parallel to the floor with palms facing forwards as you inhale through your nose.

2   Keeping your arms straight, exhale through your nose as you bring your arms together in front of your chest as if your were going to clap your hands in front of you, but do not clap them.

3   Inhale and open your arms once again to the sides and continue with a comfortable rhythm, inhaling and exhaling as you open and close your arms around your chest for 1–3 minutes.

4   Relax your arms and rest your hands in your lap.

EGO ERADICATOR POSE

Repeat the entire sequence twice, with 1–2 minutes of long and deep breathing between repeats.

1   Sit cross-legged with a straight spine and slightly tuck your chin. Curl your fingers so that the tips touch the top of the palm. Point your thumbs outwards. Straighten your arms and lift them to a 60-degree angle from the floor.

2   With your eyes closed and focusing on your mind's eye, begin inhaling and exhaling through the nose in short, rapid breaths for 1–3 minutes.

3   End by inhaling and holding your breath for ten seconds as you raise your arms above your head, touching the tips of your thumbs together and straightening out your fingers. Exhale and allow your arms to sweep downwards on either side of you and rest your hands in your lap.

Step 1

PADMA MUDRA

Hold the mudra and continue the meditation for at least 2–3 minutes and for up to 10 minutes.

1   Sit cross-legged with a straight spine and hands together in front of your chest. Press the base of the palms together and keep the little fingers and thumbs touching as you spread the remaining fingers away from each other.

2   As you hold the mudra in front of your chest, focus on your breath. Slowly inhale for five seconds, hold for five seconds and then exhale for five seconds, keeping your belly relaxed. Let your diaphragm do the work, not your abdominal muscles. Do this for ten cycles.

PADMA MUDRA

You may recite the heart chakra mantra or affirmation (see page 76) while holding the mudra.

Heart chakra
Meditations and Mantras

ASTROLOGY

LIBRA

A balanced heart chakra supports the deep Libran desire for a variety of intimate and loving friendships and relationships.

TAURUS

A balanced heart chakra supports the Taurean need to be grounded in reality and serves to remind them to want what they have.

Using meditation and mantras on the heart chakra can be heart opening. Focusing your attention on the centre of your heart will create feelings of self-acceptance and deep compassion for others. Holding the open heart space will provide you with the energy needed to generate deep gratitude and empathy for others.

While you meditate, you can recite affirmations aloud and focus on your breathing, or you can repeat a mantra in your mind for a few minutes while you quietly sit still in your meditation.

Begin long and deep breathing and begin to visualize chakra balancing energy spinning at the centre of your chest. Using your mind's eye, 'see' the colour green spinning in your heart. This is the source of your ability to love and to heal. Allow this energy to generate gratitude with great compassion for yourself and great empathy for others.

MANTRA: YAM

Yam focuses your intention on the love and acceptance of yourself and others. Meditating while chanting 'yam' helps remind you of your value and strengthens your ability to forgive yourself and others. It will provide you with a great capacity for love to balance and energize the upper chakras.

AFFIRMATION

'My heart chakra is my fourth energy centre and it functions to provide me with empathy and compassion towards others.

It is the source of my ability to heal others and myself and to send and receive love. My heart wisdom is known here.'

76

Heart chakra
Diet

TINCTURES

Hawthorn berry tincture supports the heart chakra and may help you to cultivate self-love and encourage you to follow your heart.

The heart chakra is fuelled by foods that support empathy and compassion. The focus is on green-coloured foods, vegetables, spices and teas. These foods help to open our hearts with vibrant energy from leafy greens and enable us to give and receive love. Consuming foods that support the heart chakra facilitates our ability to be generous, accepting and to break bread with others.

The following are suggestions for foods that can be incorporated into your diet for optimum heart chakra health and vitality.

Vegetables: Spinach, kale, dandelion leaves, broccoli, cauliflower, celery, cabbage, squash

Herbs: Basil, sage, thyme, coriander, parsley, rosemary

Liquids: Green teas

TEAS

Select one or more of the
heart chakra balancing
herbs and brew them with
sacred intention to support
circulation and heart
function. These teas calm
and warm the heart
and help you feel deep
gratitude and compassion.

- Hawthorn berry
- Lavender
- Sweet basil
- Jasmine
- Marjoram
- Thyme (left)

Heart chakra
Reiki

Step 1

Step 2

Reiki subtle energy can be beneficial for balancing the heart chakra. Focusing your intention on the pump of life will provide you with an open and compassionate love consciousness.

Use the heart chakra meditation (see page 76) and visualize the reiki universal life energy flowing as you hold these hand positions. You may do this sitting upright in a chair with your feet flat on the ground.

1   Close your eyes and cup your hands. With your palms facing you and the tips of your middle fingers touching, place your hands on your chest. Gently press your fingers on the middle part of your sternum.

2   Place your hands behind you, on the middle part of your shoulders with your fingertips facing downwards and inwards, towards your spine. Gently press your fingers on your shoulders.

Hold each hand position and continue the meditation for 2–3 minutes. Begin long and deep breathing as you visualize the reiki universal life energy flowing from the palms of your hands towards the centre of your body.

Visualize the colour green spinning in your heart. This is the point at which your upper and lower chakras are balanced and integrated. Your ability to have compassion and gratitude are sourced here. Allow this energy to generate great compassion for yourself and great empathy for others.

The sweet, pungent and citrus smells combine to open your heart chakra to experience the joy of gratitude, compassion and forgiveness. Dilute by mixing 1–2 drops of one or more of these essential oils with 5–6 drops of coconut oil. Rub this on the soles of your feet or the back of your neck, or externally at the point of the chakra.

- Geranium
- Bergamot
- Rose
- Melissa (left)

Heart chakra
Crystals

COLOUR THERAPY

GREEN

The frequency of the colour green is in harmony with the frequency of the heart chakra. Whether it is a green object or a green light, the heart chakra will be affected. Green signifies vital life forces of great love and compassion.

The frequency and resonance of heart chakra crystals can help open the gates to compassion and gratitude. This is the chakra of love and acceptance and both the energetic resonance of the musical note F and the colour green enhance the frequencies of heart chakra crystals.

The heart chakra can be influenced by the energetic frequencies of any of the following crystals:

- Rose quartz
- Jade
- Bloodstone
- Green calcite

Choose one or more of the crystals for balancing the heart chakra. Simply hold the crystals in your left hand. Use the heart chakra meditation (see page 76) for 3–5 minutes to send healing energy from the crystal to the heart chakra energy centre. During your meditations, visualize the colour green and use recorded music or videos that support heart chakra balancing.

SOUND THERAPY

NOTE F

Crystal bowls, singing bowls, tuning forks and gongs tuned to the note F can be used alongside crystals to balance the heart chakra. The note F will help create a sense of empathy and generosity.

ABOVE (FROM TOP): Green calcite, bloodstone, jade and rose quartz are all crystals associated with healing and unblocking the heart chakra. To determine which ones work best for you, try out a couple and trust your intuition.

Throat Chakra

The throat or *vishuddha* chakra is the fifth of the seven chakras and the first of three spiritual chakras. It is the energetic source of your 'voice' and governs your ability to share yourself with the world.

THROAT CHAKRA

The throat chakra is located in the centre of the neck, between the throat and spine.

The throat chakra is the source of your self-expression. This energy centre provides you with the power of communication. It functions to connect and balance the thoughts of the mind with the feelings of the heart. It assists in your ability to know when to speak and when to listen. When properly developed, you are able to share your thoughts and feelings with others to create a life you love. Your truth and authenticity are revealed as you share and inspire others.

The throat chakra translates your feelings and emotions into words and links you to the spiritual world through the fifth of the five Ayurvedic tattvas (elements), ether. This chakra has an energetic colour of light blue and is symbolized by the sixteen-petal lotus.

BALANCED / UNBALANCED CONDITIONS

With a balanced fifth chakra you have confidence and feel understood and seen in the world, which enables you to be fully self-expressed.

Imbalances in the fifth chakra may leave you reluctant or unable to speak your truth. You may also make things up to avoid having to tell the truth. If you were told to be 'seen and not heard', you may be left feeling shut down and silenced, and unable to express yourself. The resulting anxiety may leave you feeling isolated and unseen.

If the throat chakra is overactive, you may speak before thinking. You may get very creative in trying to deceive others and believe that you are telling the truth as long as you are not lying. You may be loud and insistent, and find it very hard to stop and listen, and instead speak non-stop about trivial matters. Gossiping and being a know-it-all may be prevalent. Silence in a conversation may be unbearable.

If the throat chakra is underactive, you may be extremely shy, petrified to speak in public and unable to have a one-on-one conversation. You want to share an idea, but just cannot conjure up the nerve to speak. When you do speak, you may be unsure and timid, and unable to communicate your thoughts, ideas or feelings effectively, and end up feeling misunderstood and unheard.

Throat chakra
The Body

BODY PARTS

- Jaw
- Mouth
- Larynx
- Trachea
- Throat
- Neck
- Brainstem

ENDOCRINE GLANDS

Thyroid – regulates
body temperature
and metabolism.

The major body systems associated with the throat chakra are:

- **Respiratory system:** Throat, pharynx, trachea
- **Circulatory system:** Carotid arteries, jugular veins
- **Nervous system:** Cerebellum, spinal cord, vagus nerve, autonomic nervous system
- **Musculoskeletal system:** Tongue, trapezius, hyoid bone, cervical spine.
- **Endocrine system:** Thyroid
- **Gastrointestinal system:** Mouth, teeth, salivary glands, epiglottis, oesophagus
- **Immune system:** Thyroid, tonsils, lymph vessels, lymph nodes, adenoids

The throat chakra is located at the centre of the neck near the cervical spine and affects the mouth, jaw, teeth, tongue, throat, eustachian tubes, voice box, epiglottis and cervical spine. This is where anything that is put into the body is controlled and regulated. Eating, breathing, swallowing, tasting and speaking all happen with great precision and with relatively little conscious effort.

The throat chakra energetically supports the gateway for respiration and the gastrointestinal system. A balanced throat chakra helps ensure that food enters the body in a way that can be utilized for proper nutrition. The epiglottis effortlessly determines whether air or food is entering the body and opens and closes the appropriate pathway for inhalation or ingestion. The larynx, or voice box, provides the instrument of communication that allows self-expression through speaking, singing, humming and even shouting.

Maintaining a balanced throat chakra assures that the portal to the outside world is open and available for clear communication and the consumption of air and food. Keeping the throat chakra energized and vital will help you receive the necessary components for life and provide a mechanism for speaking and hearing your truth.

THYROID GLAND AND THE HEART CHAKRA

A balanced throat chakra helps the thyroid produce hormones that regulate the metabolism of all cells in the body. Thyroxine (T4) and triiodothyronine (T3) are the primary hormones produced by the thyroid gland. T3 is the active hormone that affects how the body metabolizes the nutrients that are provided to each cell. T4 is made available to be converted to T3 if needed. The thyroid works in concert with the pituitary gland and the hypothalamus gland to stimulate or inhibit the production of T3 and T4. Maintaining this delicate balance ensures that calories are efficiently burned within each cell. A healthy and vital thyroid gland ensures the optimum function of cells to properly manage weight and overall energy levels.

Throat chakra
Ayurvedic/Kundalini

COBRA POSE

Step 2

The throat chakra is the first spiritual energy centre of the upper triangle of kundalini energy flow. It is where the energies of the lower triangle are accumulated and expressed. This energy centre is associated with the fifth Ayurvedic tattva (element), ether, and is where the Ayurvedic nadis (energy channels) intersect at the centre of the neck. Maintaining flexibility, balance and range of motion in the neck provides a clear opening for powerful communication.

Practising these kundalini yoga poses will fortify the throat chakra. Using the mudra (hand position) during meditation will help to clear and open the throat chakra.

COBRA POSE

Repeat the entire sequence twice, with 1–2 minutes of long and deep breathing between repeats.

1 Lie face down on your mat with your palms flat on the mat next to your shoulders.

2 Keep the tops of your feet, legs and pelvis on the mat. Slowly inhale as you gently press your pelvis into the mat and begin to lift your chest off the floor using the muscles of your lower back. Keep your elbows partially bent with your head held high.

3 Keep your gaze directly in front and feel your spine lengthening, as you draw your shoulders down, not back. Gently exhale as you bring your chest back down to the mat.

4 Repeat the pose ten times, breathing long and deep for each inhale up and each exhale down.

SHOULDER SHRUG POSE

Repeat the entire sequence twice, with 1 minute of long and deep breathing between repeats.

1   Sit cross-legged with a straight spine and hold your knees with your hands.

2   Inhale and lift your shoulders up towards your ears (A), then allow them to drop as you exhale (B). Continue to lift and drop your shoulders as you inhale and exhale and slowly begin to increase the speed of the rhythm.

3   Find a speed that is comfortable for you and continue for 1–2 minutes.

SHOULDER SHRUG POSE

Step 2A

Step 2B

DHARMA MUDRA

Hold the mudra and continue the meditation for at least 2–3 minutes and for up to 10 minutes.

1   Sit cross-legged with a straight spine and interlace your fingers on the inside of your hands. Let the tips of your thumbs touch and point them upwards, making a circle with your thumbs and index fingers.

2   As you hold the mudra in front of your navel, focus on your breath. Slowly inhale for five seconds, hold for five seconds and then exhale for five seconds, keeping your belly relaxed. Let your diaphragm do the work, not your abdominal muscles. Do this for ten cycles.

DHARMA MUDRA

You may recite the throat chakra mantra or affirmation (see page 90) while holding the mudra.

Throat chakra
Meditations and Mantras

ASTROLOGY

GEMINI

A balanced throat chakra supports the Geminian desire to feel understood and seen in the world.

VIRGO

A balanced throat chakra provides Virgoans with the gift of asking for what they want and getting it.

Using meditation and mantras on the throat chakra can build self-confidence to be fully self-expressed. Focusing your attention on the centre of your neck will connect you to the world through your voice. Place sacred intention on your throat chakra to provide the energy needed to see and feel seen in the world so that you can be of service to others.

While you meditate, you can recite affirmations aloud and focus on your breathing, or you can repeat a mantra in your mind for a few minutes while you quietly sit still in your meditation.

Begin long and deep breathing and begin to visualize chakra balancing energy spinning at the centre of your neck. Using your mind's eye, 'see' the colour light blue spinning between your throat and your spine. Allow this energy to provide you with the ability to fully express yourself with clarity and confidence.

MANTRA: HAM

Ham opens the lines of communication, both physically and spiritually. Meditating while chanting 'ham' helps you to express yourself clearly with others and with your requests to the universe. It will provide powerful and clear communication while sharing your thoughts and ideas in private or public speaking.

AFFIRMATION

'My throat chakra is my fifth energy centre and it functions to provide me with the ability to powerfully communicate with others.

It is the source of my self-expression and allows me to share my gifts with the world.'

Throat chakra
Diet

TINCTURES

Red clover blossom
tincture supports the
throat chakra and can
help you to surrender
trapped energy that needs
to be communicated.

The throat chakra is fuelled by foods that provide energy and
a variety of tastes that reflect our complex nature. Natural
sugars from sweet fruit, sour from citrus fruit and salty
spices are stimulating and fuel clarity of communication.
Consuming foods that support the throat chakra facilitates
our ability to be delightful and engaged in social situations.

The following are suggestions for foods that can be
incorporated into your diet for optimum throat chakra
health and vitality.

Fruit: Lemons, limes, grapefruit, kiwi, apples, pears, plums,
peaches, apricots

Seasoning/herbs: Sea salt, lemongrass

Liquids: Water, 100 per cent fruit juices (no added sugar),
herbal teas

Select one or more of the
throat chakra balancing
herbs and brew them with
sacred intention to support
respiratory health and
clear communication.
These teas open the throat
and provide the breath
support that will help
you express yourself
powerfully to others.

• Sage
• Lemongrass (left)
• Mullein leaf

Throat chakra
Reiki

Step 1

Step 2

Reiki subtle energy can be beneficial for balancing the throat chakra. Focusing your intention on the power you have to share your ideas will provide you with the confidence to pursue any project or goal.

Use the throat chakra meditation (see page 90) and visualize the reiki universal life energy flowing as you hold these hand positions. You may do this sitting upright in a chair with your feet flat on the ground.

1   Close your eyes and cup your hands. Place your hands at the front of your throat, with the base of your palms touching. Hover your hands beneath your jaw.

2   Close your eyes and place your hands on the back of your skull. Touch your index and middle fingers together. Hover your hands over the back and lower part of your skull.

Hold each hand position and continue the meditation for 2–3 minutes. Begin long and deep breathing as you visualize the reiki universal life energy flowing from the palms of your hands towards the centre of your neck.

Visualize the colour light blue spinning between your throat and spine. This is the megaphone of your self-expression. Your ability to communicate with others is sourced here. Allow this energy to give you the ability to fully express yourself with clarity and confidence.

Meld soothing, cleansing, warm and bright scents to open your throat chakra and support clear speaking and keen listening. Dilute by mixing 1–2 drops of one or more of these essential oils with 5–6 drops of coconut oil. Rub this on the soles of your feet or the back of your neck, or externally at the point of the chakra.

- Peppermint
- Blue camomile (left)
- Sage
- Geranium
- Myrrh
- Sandalwood

Throat chakra
Crystals

COLOUR THERAPY

LIGHT BLUE

The frequency of the colour light blue is in harmony with the frequency of the throat chakra. Whether it is a light blue object or a light, the throat chakra will be affected. Light blue signifies calm, clear and confident communication.

The frequency and resonance of throat chakra crystals support powerful communication energy. This is the chakra of clear self-expression and sharing of ideas. Both the energetic resonance of the musical note G and the colour light blue enhance the frequencies of throat chakra crystals.

The throat chakra can be influenced by the energetic frequencies of any of the following crystals:

- Aquamarine
- Turquoise
- Lapis lazuli
- Blue topaz

Choose one or more of the crystals for balancing the throat chakra. Simply hold the crystal in your left hand. Use the throat chakra meditation (see page 90) for 3–5 minutes to send healing energy from the crystal to the throat chakra energy centre. During your meditations, visualize the colour light blue and use recorded music or videos that support throat chakra balancing.

SOUND THERAPY

NOTE G

Crystal bowls, singing
bowls, tuning forks and
gongs tuned to the note G
can be used alongside
crystals to balance the
throat chakra. The note G
will help create a sense
of being seen and
understood in the world.

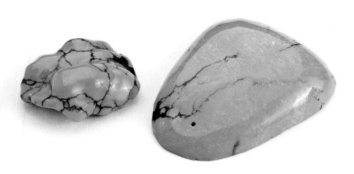

ABOVE (FROM TOP): Aquamarine, turquoise and
lapis lazuli are all crystals associated with
healing and unblocking the throat chakra.
To determine which ones work best for you,
try out a couple and trust your intuition.

Third Eye Chakra

The third eye or *ajna* chakra is the sixth of the seven chakras and the second of three spiritual chakras. It is the source of your spiritual insight and intuition, and the gateway to higher consciousness.

THIRD EYE CHAKRA

The third eye chakra is located just above the eyebrows in the centre of the forehead.

The third eye chakra is beyond the physical world. This energy centre provides you with the ability to be introspective. It functions to reveal your highest truth and leads you to trust in yourself. It provides you with the ability to see the context of situations and develop your emotional intelligence. When properly developed, you have a higher overall perspective and are able to more keenly consider your options and choose powerfully.

The third eye chakra is connected to all of the five Ayurvedic tattvas (elements) and provides context by revealing the seen along with the unseen. This chakra has an energetic colour of indigo and is symbolized by two petals on each side of a central circle.

BALANCED / UNBALANCED CONDITIONS

With a balanced sixth chakra you have clarity and awareness that can provide you with insight into your past, present and future.

Imbalances in the sixth chakra may leave you narrow-minded and unable to make decisions because of a lack of clarity. You may ignore information that is in plain sight and be unable to focus on your goal. You may appear confused or out-of-it to others, without realizing it yourself. Your lack of self-knowledge may compromise your ability to empathize with others.

**If the third eye
chakra is overactive,**
you may have
nightmares,
visions or psychic
disturbances. You may
suffer from delusions
and move through the
world always in your head,
and have difficulty grounding
yourself. Being lost in your
thoughts, you may be unable to
connect with others in a deep
and meaningful way.

If the third eye chakra is underactive,
you may have trouble trusting your intuition.
Poor memory and disorientation may leave you unable to see the path
you are on or the direction you are going in life. Rather than learning
from your experiences, you may repeat the same mistakes over and
over, expecting a different result.

Third eye chakra
The Body

BODY PARTS

- Face
- Nose
- Eyes
- Ears
- Sinuses
- Brain
- Skull

ENDOCRINE GLANDS

Pituitary gland – produces hormones that govern the function of the previous five glands.

Pineal gland – this is sometimes linked to the third eye chakra in addition to the crown chakra (see page 114).

The major body systems associated with the third eye chakra are:

- **Nervous system:** Cerebral cortex

- **Musculoskeletal system:** Cranium, facial bones

- **Endocrine system:** Pituitary, pineal

The third eye chakra is located just above the bridge of the nose, between the eyebrows, and physically affects the sinuses and eyes. This is where you are physically clear-headed and can interpret the actual images perceived with your eyes to imagine beyond the material world.

The third eye chakra energetically raises the vibration of your consciousness to experience beyond the three-dimensional world. A balanced third eye chakra helps ensure that we can access our higher selves, seeing beyond the personality and more deeply past the ego. This is the doorway to inner vision, insight and intuition. In meditation, placing your focus on your third eye chakra provides an opportunity for stillness of body and mind that is conducive to insight and introspection. Your inner truth, purpose and intentions are revealed here.

Maintaining a balanced third eye chakra assures that you are clear in your goals and aware of opportunities when they are presented. Keeping the third eye chakra energized and vital will help you achieve mystical states of consciousness, and receive wisdom to guide you through your life and to trust your intuition.

PITUITARY GLAND AND
THE THIRD EYE CHAKRA

A balanced third eye chakra helps the
pituitary regulate the production of
hormones that regulate the function
of other endocrine glands and control
the growth of tissues and organs. The
pituitary gland is known as the master
gland because it secretes hormones
into the bloodstream that regulate
the glands of the endocrine system.
It secretes everything from human
growth hormone, which carefully
regulates the rate of growth of children
into adulthood, to LH (luteinizing
hormone) for oestrogen and
testosterone production in the gonads,
and FSH (follicle-stimulating hormone),
which regulates the maturation of the
germ cells (sexually reproductive cells).
It also affects aspects of metabolism,
pregnancy, body temperature, blood
pressure and salt concentration.
The production of endorphins for pain,
ACTH (adrenocorticotropic hormone)
in the adrenals and TSH (thyroid
stimulating hormone) for the thyroid
gland all depend on the pituitary gland
for optimum functionality. A healthy
and vital pituitary gland is critical
for a balanced and healthy body,
mind and spirit.

Third eye chakra
Ayurvedic/Kundalini

NECK ROLL POSE

Step 2A

Step 2B

Step 2C

Step 2D

The third eye chakra is the second spiritual energy centre of the upper triangle of kundalini energy flow. The energy accumulated from the previous five chakras now vibrates at a frequency high enough to look inwards and 'see' the truth of your higher self. Because this is a higher frequency energy centre that belongs in the subtle realm of spiritual energy, there is no individual Ayurvedic tattva (element) associated with it. The third eye chakra is where the Ayurvedic nadis (energy channels) intersect at the centre of the head just above and between the eyebrows. Focusing the mind between the brows will facilitate your ability to imagine and dream to create a vision of your future self.

Practising the following kundalini yoga poses will fortify the third eye chakra. Using the mudra (hand position) during meditation will help to cleanse and clear the third eye chakra.

NECK ROLL POSE

Repeat the entire sequence twice, with 1 minute of long and deep breathing between repeats.

1   Sit cross-legged with a straight spine and hands on knees, inhaling deeply and slowly. Lengthen your neck and relax your shoulders.

2   Lengthen your neck backwards (A) and then begin rotating to the left in a clockwise direction. Exhale slowly as your left ear passes over your left shoulder (B), tuck your chin towards your chest as you drop your head forwards (C) and then inhale slowly as your right ear passes over your right shoulder (D). Finish to the back again.

3   Continue this rotation for 1–2 minutes, then repeat anticlockwise for 1–2 minutes.

GURU PRANAM POSE

Repeat the entire sequence twice, with 1 minute of normal breathing between repeats.

Step 2

1   Kneel on your mat with knees hip-width apart and the top of your feet flat on the mat with big toes almost touching each other. Sit back onto your heels, then lean forwards with chest on thighs and rest your forehead on the mat.

2   Stretch your arms above your head with palms and fingers touching. Begin long and deep breathing through your nose, slowly inhaling for five seconds, then exhaling for five seconds.

3   Continue for ten breaths. Feel the pressure of your forehead on the mat and the stretch along your spine and the opening between your 'sit bones' as you allow the perineum (between the genitals and anus) to relax.

KALESVARA MUDRA

Hold the mudra and continue the meditation for at least 2–3 minutes and for up to 10 minutes.

KALESVARA MUDRA

You may recite the third eye chakra mantra or affirmation (see page 104) while holding the mudra.

1   Sit cross-legged with a straight spine. Touch the tips of your middle fingers together and also your thumbs. Bend the remaining fingers and press the second knuckles and phalanges of each finger together.

2   As you hold the mudra above your navel with your middle fingers pointing upwards, focus on your breath. Slowly inhale for five seconds, hold for five seconds and then exhale for five seconds, keeping your belly relaxed. Let your diaphragm do the work, not your abdominal muscles. Do this for ten cycles.

Third eye chakra
Meditations and Mantras

ASTROLOGY

CANCER

A balanced third eye chakra provides Cancerians with insight into their past, present and future.

Using meditation and mantras on the third eye chakra can provide feelings of connection to your highest self. Focusing your attention on the centre of your head, looking inwards, will help you see your truth. Place sacred intention on your third eye chakra to provide the energy needed for clarity in decision-making and understanding to live a joyful life so that you can be of service to others.

While you meditate, you can recite affirmations aloud and focus on your breathing, or you can repeat a mantra in your mind for a few minutes while you quietly sit still in your meditation.

Begin long and deep breathing and begin to visualize chakra balancing energy spinning between your eyebrows at the base of your forehead. Using your mind's eye, 'see' the colour indigo spinning behind your eyebrows at the centre of your head. Allow this energy to provide you with the ability to see beyond the physical and trust your intuition.

MANTRA: AUM

Aum cleanses the third eye for clarity of intuitive vision. Meditating while chanting 'aum' helps provide access to your inner wisdom. With a clear third eye chakra, you can trust your inner voice and know that you are proceeding on the path that is best for you.

AFFIRMATION

'My third eye chakra is my sixth energy centre and it functions to provide me with insight and intuition.

It is the source of my "sixth sense" and allows me to see others and myself as we really are.'

Third eye chakra
Diet

Eyebright tincture supports the third eye chakra and can enable you to see the truth clearly with a calm, objective eye.

The third eye chakra is fuelled by foods that are nutrient dense and provide high frequency energy to our bodies. Eating purple fruits that are antioxidants and drinking fruit juices that are detoxifying increase clarity of vision. Consuming foods that support the third eye chakra facilitates the awareness needed to develop and trust your intuition.

The following are suggestions for foods that can be incorporated into your diet for optimum third eye chakra health and vitality.

Fruit: Blueberries, blackberries, raspberries, cranberries, goji berries, red grapes, acai, pomegranates

Flavourings/herbs: Lavender, mugwort

Liquids: Red wine, 100 per cent grape juice (no added sugar)

Nuts/seeds: Raw walnuts, sprouted almonds, poppy seeds

Select one or more of the third eye chakra balancing herbs and brew them with sacred intention to support your vision and intuition. These teas enhance the ability to focus and make decisions by clarifying and calming the mind.

- Gotu kola
- Lavender (left, with camomile)

Third eye chakra
Reiki

Step 1

Step 2

Reiki subtle energy can be beneficial for balancing the third eye chakra. Focusing your intention on your ability to see and know who you are will provide you with the knowledge to understand what service you have to offer to others.

Use the third eye chakra meditation (see page 104) and visualize the reiki universal life energy flowing as you hold these hand positions. You may do this sitting upright in a chair with your feet flat on the ground.

1   Close your eyes and cup your hands. Hover your hands over your eyes. With your fingertips, lightly touch the top of your forehead.

2   Close your eyes and cup your hands. Hover your hands over your temples/ears. With your fingertips, lightly touch the top of your head.

Hold each hand position and continue the meditation for 2–3 minutes. Begin long and deep breathing as you visualize the reiki universal life energy flowing from the palms of your hands towards the centre of your head.

Visualize the colour indigo spinning behind your eyebrows at the centre of your head. This is your access point to inner vision. Your ability to connect with your higher self is sourced here. Allow this energy to provide you with the ability to see beyond the physical and trust your intuition.

A combination of cooling
pine and sweet, pungent
oils provide a mesmerizing
energy that lifts you up
into the etheric realms to
access your highest self.
Dilute by mixing 1–2 drops
of one or more of these
essential oils with
5–6 drops of coconut oil.
Rub this on the soles of
your feet or the back of
your neck, or externally at
the point of the chakra.

- Marjoram
- Jasmine
- Rosemary
- Juniper (left)
- Pine
- Helichrysum

Third eye chakra
Crystals

COLOUR THERAPY

INDIGO

The frequency of the colour indigo is in harmony with the frequency of the third eye chakra. Whether it is an indigo object or an indigo light, the third eye chakra will be affected. Indigo signifies spiritual insight and intuitive truth.

The frequency and resonance of third eye chakra crystals support a spiritual state of mind. This is the chakra of intuition and highest truth. Both the energetic resonance of the musical note A and the colour indigo enhance the frequencies of third eye chakra crystals.

The third eye chakra can be influenced by the energetic frequencies of any of the following crystals:

- Amethyst
- Lepidolite
- Purple fluorite
- Azurite

Choose one or more of the crystals for balancing the third eye chakra. Simply hold the crystal in your left hand. Use the third eye chakra meditation (see page 104) for 3–5 minutes to send healing energy from the crystal to the third eye chakra energy centre. During your meditations, visualize the colour indigo and use recorded music or videos that support third eye chakra balancing.

SOUND THERAPY

NOTE A

Crystal bowls, singing bowls, tuning forks and gongs tuned to the note A can be used alongside crystals to balance the third eye chakra. The note A will help create a sense of trust to believe what you know is true.

ABOVE (FROM TOP): Lepidolite, azurite and purple fluorite are all crystals associated with healing and unblocking the third eye chakra. To determine which ones work best for you, try out a couple and trust your intuition.

Crown Chakra

The crown or *sahasrara* chakra is the seventh of the seven chakras
and the third of the three spiritual chakras. It is the point of
direct connection to your higher self and the divine.

CROWN CHAKRA

The crown chakra is
located at the top and
centre of the head.

The crown chakra is connected to the realm of the infinite
and timeless. This energy centre provides the opportunity to
experience the highest forms of consciousness. It functions
to allow feelings of joy and bliss, peace and transcendence,
and enables you to experience the mystical aspects of life.
When properly developed, you are able to know and
understand the temporary nature of all things and the
eternal nature of individual consciousness within the source
of all that is.

The crown chakra is connected to all of the five Ayurvedic
tattvas (elements) and allows you to experience the oneness
of the universe. This chakra has an energetic colour of violet
and is symbolized by the thousand-petal lotus.

BALANCED / UNBALANCED CONDITIONS

With a balanced seventh chakra you can maintain a pure
connection to the divine, which supports, balances and
energizes the entire chakra system.

Imbalances in the seventh chakra may leave you feeling
disconnected from any sort of spiritual reality. You may
move from one type of religion to another searching
for answers to spiritual questions. You may land in the
'self-help merry-go-round', applying a lot of effort to
make a connection to the divine, all to no avail.

If the crown chakra is overactive, you may experience restless thinking known as the 'monkey mind', where your thoughts overtake you and you are unable to connect or engage with those around you. You may engage in materialistic behaviour and be unable to let things go. You may hoard things or be afraid of losing them because you are overly attached to them.

If the crown chakra is underactive, you may be drawn to extremist religions to avoid having to take responsibility for your life. You may find it a relief being told what to do and how to do it. You may also revel in the world of intellectuals who base their experiences only on scientific facts and things that can be proven in the material world. All this may leave you feeling lost, alienated and spiritually disconnected.

Crown chakra
The Body

• Brain
• Skull

ENDOCRINE GLANDS

Pineal gland – regulates biological cycles, including sleep. This gland is sometimes linked to the third eye chakra as well as the crown chakra.

The major body systems associated with the crown chakra are:

• **Nervous system:** Cerebral cortex

• **Musculoskeletal system:** Frontal and parietal bones of the cranium

• **Endocrine system:** Pineal

The crown chakra is located at the top of the head and affects the brain and pineal gland. This is the least physical of all the chakras and is the direct interface between the entire physical body and the energetic body.

The crown chakra energetically holds the vibration for the optimum function of all seven chakras. This is the point at which you have access to experience beyond the physical and to feel connected to everything physical and spiritual. The sense of something much larger than your egoic-self is clear. The consciousness of yourself, other people, animals and even inanimate objects are clearly perceived as one. The sense of me and you, us and them, has no relevant meaning in this state of consciousness.

Maintaining a balanced crown chakra assures that all of the chakra energy centres are providing optimum support to all the endocrine glands and organs associated with each of the seven chakras. Keeping the crown chakra energized and vital ensures that you maintain a healthy physical body so that you can maintain a healthy spiritual body.

PINEAL GLAND AND
THE CROWN CHAKRA

A balanced crown chakra helps the pineal gland produce the hormones that regulate your circadian rhythm and the production of reproductive hormones. The hormone melatonin is produced in the pineal gland and helps ensure deep and restful sleep at night and energized alertness in the waking hours. The production of melatonin is stimulated by darkness and inhibited by light. Sensors in the retina of the eye send impulses to the pineal gland to regulate the hormone levels that in turn keep sleep patterns regular and provide you with a sense of time passing. The pineal gland also influences the pituitary gland's secretion of the sex hormones FSH (follicle-stimulating hormone) and LH (luteinizing hormone) that directly affect the development of the reproductive organs. A healthy and vital pineal gland ensures that you mature sexually, can track the passage of time and get the sleep required for optimum health and well-being.

Crown chakra
Ayurvedic/Kundalini

SAT KRIYA POSE

Step 1A

Step 1B

Place right thumb over left if you are a man, or left thumb over right if you are a woman. Straighten your index fingers upwards.

The crown chakra is the third spiritual energy centre of the upper triangle of kundalini energy flow. The highest energy frequencies of the crown chakra vibrate to illuminate your connection with the divine. Because this is a higher frequency energy centre that belongs in the subtle realm of spiritual energy, there is no individual Ayurvedic tattva (element) associated with it. The crown chakra is where the Ayurvedic nadis (energy channels) intersect at the top of the head. An open crown chakra provides deep connection and union with all things and energizes the other six chakras.

Practising the following kundalini yoga poses will fortify the crown chakra. Using the mudra (hand position) during meditation will help to open the crown chakra.

SAT KRIYA POSE

This deeply spiritual pose helps move kundalini energy up the spine through all seven chakras. Do it once.

1   Kneel with thighs touching and the top of your feet flat on your mat. Sit back onto your heels. With a straight spine, lift your arms above your head with elbows straight and next to your ears (A). Clasp your hands as shown (B).

2   With eyes closed, begin short and rapid breathing, pulling your navel quickly in towards your spine and saying 'Sat' with the inhale, then releasing your naval and saying 'Nam' with the exhale. 'SatNam' means 'Truth is my name'.

3   Find a speed that is comfortable for you and continue rhythmically for 3–11 minutes. When complete, release the pose, lie back on your mat and relax for 5 minutes.

HALF LOTUS POSE

Do this pose once, concentrating on the connection between mind, body and spirit to achieve a sense of peace and joy.

1   Sit on your mat with your legs in front of you. Bend your right leg, bringing the knee towards your chest. Bring your right ankle towards your left hip and lower your right knee to the mat. Your right foot should be at the crease of the left hip, with the bottom of your right foot facing upwards. Now bend the left leg and tuck your left ankle under your right knee. Place your hands as shown.

2   Close your eyes and do long and deep breathing for 2–3 minutes. Then repeat the pose, reversing the position of your legs. When complete, release the pose, lie back on your mat and relax for 5 minutes.

Step 1

Place your hands on your knees palm upwards, or hold them in gyan mudra (see page 33) or bring them to your chest in prayer position.

HAKINA MUDRA

It is important to have meditated with the other six mudras prior to this one. Hold this mudra and continue the meditation for at least 2–3 minutes and for up to 10 minutes.

1   Sit cross-legged with a straight spine. Touch the tips of your ring fingers together and interlace the remaining fingers with the right thumb over the left.

2   As you hold the mudra above your navel with your ring fingers pointing upwards, focus on your breath. Slowly inhale for five seconds, hold for five seconds and then exhale for five seconds, keeping your belly relaxed. Let your diaphragm do the work, not your abdominal muscles. Do this for ten cycles.

HAKINA MUDRA

You may recite the crown chakra mantra or affirmation (see page 118) while holding the mudra.

117

Crown chakra

Meditations and Mantras

ASTROLOGY

LEO

A balanced crown chakra provides Leos with the pure connection to the divine that helps them temper their fiery ambition.

Using meditation and mantras on the crown chakra can provide a powerful connection to the divine. Focusing your attention on the top of your head, looking outwards, will help you know your place in the world. Place sacred intention on your crown chakra to provide you with the energy needed to create a blissful sense of peace and well-being so that you can be of service to others.

While you meditate, you can recite affirmations aloud and focus on your breathing, or you can repeat a mantra in your mind for a few minutes while you quietly sit still in your meditation.

Begin long and deep breathing and begin to visualize chakra balancing energy spinning at the top of your head. Using your mind's eye, 'see' the colour violet spinning just above your head. Allow this energy to provide you with the ability to experience your divinity and connect to your life purpose.

MANTRA: OM

Om brings about a stillness that allows access to your highest self. Meditating while chanting 'om' helps connect you to the divine. An open and clear crown chakra brings grace to your life, allowing you to be in the moment and at peace without attachment or desire.

AFFIRMATION

'My crown chakra is my seventh energy centre and it functions to provide me with a connection to the infinite and timeless nature of the universe.

It is the source of my oneness with the divine and allows me to have a magical sense of being.'

118

Crown chakra
Diet

Lavender tincture supports the crown chakra and may help to slow the mind and enable you to receive divine guidance from the universe.

The crown chakra is highly energized and is fuelled more by intention while eating than by any particular food. Blessing food before you eat and eating consciously with gratitude creates a balanced state of mind. Incorporating intention and gratitude while you eat supports the crown chakra and facilitates the connection to the divine.

The following are suggestions that can be used for optimum crown chakra health and vitality.

Air fasting/detoxing

Incense/smudging herbs: Sage, juniper, copal, myrrh, frankincense

Note: Incense and smudging herbs are not to be eaten, but are ritually inhaled through the nostrils or can be smoked through a ceremonial pipe for purification purposes.

Select one or more of the crown chakra balancing herbs and brew them with sacred intention to support your connection with the universe. These teas raise your vibration so that you feel one with all and at peace with yourself and the world.

- Elderberry
- Angelica root
- White sage (left)

Crown chakra
Reiki

Step 1

Step 2

Reiki subtle energy can be beneficial for balancing the crown chakra. Focusing your intention on the brilliance of your internal light, sourced by the divine, will empower you to be unstoppable, inspiring and a sacred force in the world.

Use the crown chakra meditation (see page 118) and visualize the reiki universal life energy flowing as you hold these hand positions. You may do this sitting upright in a chair with your feet flat on the ground.

1   Close your eyes and cup your hands. Hover your hands over your eyes. With your fingertips, lightly touch the top of your forehead.

2   Close your eyes and cup your hands. Hover your hands over your temples/ears. With your fingertips, lightly touch the top of your head.

Hold each hand position and continue the meditation for 2–3 minutes. Begin long and deep breathing as you visualize the reiki universal life energy flowing from the palms of your hands towards the top of your head.

Visualize the colour violet spinning at the crown of your head at the top of your skull. This is your point of connection with the divine. Your ability to experience oneness with all is sourced here. Allow this energy to facilitate the experience of your own divinity and connection to the universe.

Heavenly sweetness
and rich orange and rose
scents overtake your sense
of smell as you experience
the magnificence of being
alive. Dilute by mixing
1–2 drops of one or more
of these essential oils with
5–6 drops of coconut oil.
Rub this on the soles of
your feet or the back of
your neck, or externally at
the point of the chakra.

- Frankincense
- Lotus
- Rosewood
- Jasmine
- Rose (left)
- Neroli

Crown chakra
Crystals

COLOUR THERAPY

VIOLET

The frequency of the colour violet is in harmony with the frequency of the crown chakra. Whether it is a violet object or a violet light, the crown chakra will be affected. Violet signifies direct spiritual connection and oneness with all.

The frequency and resonance of crown chakra crystals open and still the mind. This is the chakra of purity, bliss and joy, and both the energetic resonance of the musical note B and the colour violet enhance the frequencies of crown chakra crystals.

The crown chakra can be influenced by the energetic frequencies of any of the following crystals:

- Clear quartz
- Selenite
- Herkimer diamond
- Clear apophyllite

Choose one or more of the crystals for balancing the crown chakra. Simply hold the crystal in your left hand. Use the crown chakra meditation (see page 118) for 3–5 minutes to send healing energy from the crystal to the crown chakra energy centre. During your meditations, visualize the colour violet and use recorded music or videos that support crown chakra balancing.

SOUND THERAPY

NOTE B

Crystal bowls, singing bowls, tuning forks and gongs tuned to the note B can be used alongside crystals to balance the crown chakra. The note B will help create a sense of deep peace and well-being.

ABOVE (FROM TOP): Clear apophyllite, Hermiker diamonds and selenite are all crystals associated with healing and unblocking the crown chakra. To determine which ones work best for you, try out a couple and trust your intuition.

Index

Credits

Quarto would like to thank the following for supplying images reproduced in this book:

a above; b below; l left; r right; c centre

www.shutterstock.com: p.1 Zanna Art; p.2 Chris002; p.3, 9, 27 Trish Volt; p.5 Zanna Art; p.7 Asmiana; p.8 Chris002; p.10 Yellowj; p.12, 13 Zanna Art; p.15 Kite_rin; p.16 Cornelia Pithart; p.17 irin-k; p.19 Romolo Tavani; p.20 Serg64; p.21 gresei; p.22 New Africa; p.23 wavebreakmedia; p.24 Reid Dalland; p.25 luckyraccoon; p.26 An Vino; p.29, 43, 57, 71, 85, 99, 113 BigMouse; p.31 Byjeng; p.35 jonnysek-jiri; p.37 Sergii Tverdokhlibov; p.39 StockImageFactory.com; p.40 Albert Russ; p.41a Nik Merkulov; p.41c Coldmoon Photoproject; p.41b Africa Studio; p.45 Monkey Business Images; p.49 Holger Graebner; p.51 Maya Kruchankova; p.53 Madeleine Steinbach; p.54, 55a Coldmoon Photoproject; p.55c Reika; p.55b vvoe; p.59 Nenad Aksic; p.63 gornjak; p.65 Shustikova Inessa; p.67 White bear studio;

p.68 Nastya22; p.69a, 69b vvoe; p.69c Roy Palmer; p.73 mimagephotography; p.77 matthew25; p.79 Fortyforks; p.81 ulrich22; p.82 kongsky; p.83a Roy Palmer; p. 83c vvoe; p.83b Richard Peterson; p.87 mimagephotography; p.91 Dmitry Polonskiy; p.93 PhuShutter; p.95 Tatyana Vyc; p.96 Nastya22; p.97a, 97b J. Palys; p.97c Alexander Hoffmann; p.101 Antonio Guillem; p.105 guteksk7; p.107 CoralAntlerCreative; p.109 Melica; p.110 Albert Russ; p.111a Coldmoon Photoproject; p.111c Dafinchi; p.111b olpo; p.115 Stock-Asso; p.119 Praew stock; p.121 Insolite; p.123 gowithstock; p.124 bjphotographs; p.125a Nastya22; p.125c Bjoern Wylezich; p.125b Tamara Kulikova.

All other photographs and illustrations are the copyright of Quarto Publishing plc. While every effort has been made to credit contributors, Quarto would like to apologize should there have been any omissions or errors – and would be pleased to make the appropriate correction for future editions of the book.

AUTHOR'S ACKNOWLEDGEMENTS

The myriad systems that influence and are influenced by the chakras clearly emphasizes the role these active energy centres play in our lives. The chakras literally form the backbone for our wellness. Writing this book has provided me with a deeper appreciation of the world in which we live.

I would like to acknowledge you, the reader, for embracing your well-being in a proactive way. Thank you!

Once again, I'd like to thank the publishing team who has provided the much needed support in the quest to present this complex subject in a simple and elegant way. Kudos to the team for their expertise and professionalism.

Finally, a huge appreciation for my husband, Steven, who creates the space for me to pursue my passion for wellness and sharing knowledge with others.